Disability and the Problem of Evil

Zachary D. Schmoll

 Public Philosophy Press

Published by Public Philosophy Press 2021

Phoenix, Arizona

www.publicphilosophypress.com

Cover design by Virginia De La Lastra

First edition

ISBN: 978-1-7365424-4-6 (paper)

Endorsements

"*Disability and the Problem of Evil* is a gracious and concise treatment of an incredibly sensitive issue. Written from an insider's perspective, it offers valuable personal insights without sacrificing objectivity in the philosophical aspects of the discussion. Schmoll has given us a wonderful tool for improving our thinking and conversations on the problem of evil and suffering, and I expect it will also be a tremendous blessing to individuals seeking a better theological understanding of their own disability or that of a loved one."

Melissa Cain Travis, Ph.D., Affiliate Faculty, Colorado Christian University

"Books on the problem of evil abound, and it is doubtful any will ever surpass C. S. Lewis's *The Problem of Pain*. But in *Disability and the Problem of Evil*, Zak Schmoll makes a significant contribution to the discussion. Suffering from a debilitating disease that has confined him to a wheelchair, Schmoll offers a treatment that views the problem of evil from the standpoint of disability. His own history gives him a fresh perspective as he surveys the standard approaches to see if he can justify belief in a good and omnipotent God in a world containing disability. He concludes that 'for the Christian, the ultimate hope of the world was delivered in the person of Jesus Christ. Being a member of the human race, a privileged species created in the image of God, with the ability to have a relationship with our Creator, is a blessing unsurpassed in the remainder of the universe.' If you want to see a credible way to get to that place without closing your eyes to the reality of disability in this world, this is a book you will definitely want to read."

Donald T. Williams, Ph.D., Professor Emeritus, Toccoa Falls College, Past President, International Society of Christian Apologetics

"In his valuable book, Dr. Schmoll tackles an underexamined aspect of problem of evil. He helps us understand disability personally and theologically in order to see how God is good to us despite the prevalence of evil. This is an important contribution to the theodicy conversation."

Phil Tallon, Ph.D. Dean, School of Christian Thought, Houston Baptist University

"Do we really need another book on the problem of evil? When it is discussed within the context of disabilities, there is a great need. Some see the existence of human disabilities as refuting the idea of an all-powerful and all-good God. Zachary Schmoll comes at this question with both a keen theological mind and as a person with lived experience of a disability. He convincingly demonstrates that both the traditional conception of God and the existence of human disabilities are completely compatible."

Stephen J. Bedard, Pastor, Queen Street Baptist Church, St. Catherines, Ontario, Author of *How to Make Your Church Autism-Friendly*

Table of Contents

Introduction

On August 15, 2019, I received some news with life-altering repercussions. On that date, I received insurance approval to receive Spinraza, the first promising treatment for my condition, spinal muscular atrophy (SMA). This disability is characterized by severe and progressive muscle weakness, and this medication, administered through a lumbar puncture, slows down that deterioration. Later that night, I did what I usually do when I am trying to process something: I started writing. I wrote:

I have lived the past 28 years without the prospect for any type of meaningful treatment. You obviously do what you can. I get stretched out every day. We go to the swimming pool to try to help my flexibility and mobility. I know some people do much more intensive physical therapy regimens than I have ever done. However, all of this largely delays the inevitable, knowing that the decline is going to continue at 3%-5% every year. Not to come back to this point again, but it blows my mind to think that there may be a potential option to remove this reality from my mind. That is what I have been feeling for most of the afternoon and night. It really is a paradigm shift from where I am used to being.

Frankly, it is making me look at SMA differently. Again, I'm not delusional. I know my life will probably change very little, if any, from the results of these injections. I know that. But that's the point. Change for someone with SMA is almost always negative. You very rarely, if ever, get better. The fact that change can be slowed and ideally held at bay is unbelievably huge.

I received my first injection in January 2020 and now have made it through more than a year of treatment. My initial prognosis was largely accurate. I have not received any miraculous results, but I have seen minor increases. It seems like, at a minimum, the decline has indeed slowed down, and that's a great thing. Since being diagnosed at eighteen months, my life has been a cycle of treatments addressing problems as they occur. I received my wheelchair when I was three years old since I couldn't walk. I had spinal fusion surgery at eight years old to correct severe scoliosis. I have gone from one treatment to another, addressing problems as they occur rather than preemptively preventing issues from occurring in the first place.

The night after my first injection, January 20, 2020, I took to my computer again and tried to lay out some of my feelings. Again, I was amazed that there was finally a treatment that allowed me to go on the offensive against SMA. I still can't get over that, even to this day. I wrote this that first night:

> The bottom line, however, is that it is really interesting to be in a position to evaluate your life based on the time in which you were born, something you had no control over whatsoever. You could easily say that I am lucky to have been born when I was. I don't really think that luck had anything to do with it.

> I don't know the entire reason why, but I don't think that God made a mistake putting me in this time and place. Do I know exactly all the reasons for why I was put here and so many other people throughout the centuries have not? I don't have that information. The information I do have is that because I am here, it is vital for me to do what I can to bring glory to God in whatever way I can.

In the midst of all of this joy and excitement, there was a voice in the back of my head. I don't think I am the only one with a disability who has ever felt this way. You sometimes just want to ask, "Why?" As a Christian with a disability, that question is slightly expanded, "Why, God?" It is not a question of abandoning my faith or anything like that, but it is more a question of wanting answers. I like answers, and it is frustrating when they are not clear. There have been definite seasons where I wrestle with why disabilities exist and precisely why I have to live with my disability.

There are challenges all people must overcome. Some of those problems stem from individual choices. When someone does something risky, there is a chance of injury. When someone cheats on a test, there is a chance that he or she will be caught and given a failing grade. Neither decision had to be made, but because they were, consequences followed, in this case, these wrong actions. Those consequences make life difficult. It is hard to get into a prestigious university with a black mark of academic dishonesty on a transcript. It is hard to drive a car to work with a broken leg after a failed skateboard trick.

On the other hand, some difficulties are not directly related to individual actions. When a hurricane slams the coast of Florida, there does not seem to be any specific action that brought about the consequences of devastation following that storm. When an outbreak of a particular strain of influenza ravages a nation, some sanitation and public health decisions can be made to contain the virus, but, by and large, assigning individual blame for the initial outbreak is impossible.

There seems to be a fundamental disconnect between these types of problems. One seems to follow directly from individual action while the other seems to almost happen by random chance. One is clearly within human control while the other one is imposed on us. The first seems like the natural consequence of the law of cause and effect, while the second happens to us. One result is simpler to pin to a specific action while the other feels much more speculative. All of them are difficult, some might label all of them as evil, but they are of different kinds.

Disability, the focus of this book, has the potential to fall into both of these categories. Some disabilities develop through decisions that people make, while others develop naturally. There are no "better" or "worse"disabilities. Instead, it is critical to recognize that disability is complicated. It cannot be trivialized by trying to impose a kind of one-size-fits-all approach to its understanding. It is simply a matter of fact that different types of disabilities stem from diverse causes.

Some people do make decisions that lead to injuries. The connection between personal evil and its consequences is straightforward. Some parents make decisions that affect their children's mental health, so disability can stem from the evil choices of some people that impact other people as well. The connection is relatively straightforward between personal evil and its consequences, but the victim of the evil had no choice in the matter. Some people are born with genetic conditions that they had no control over. Beyond the simple fact of two people with perhaps unknown genetic predispositions choosing to have a child, there were no choices that can directly connect to the presence of a disability in this situation. Therefore, when the skeptical world asks why God doesn't heal all disabilities, there is no simple answer to that question. Even at this early point in our discussion, it should be evident that if God were to heal all disabilities, He would need to act in various ways to achieve this goal. Could God impede our free will so that we don't make decisions that lead to injuries? Sometimes that would prevent an injury that leads to a disability. Does God have to intervene in the creation of our genetic code and prevent genetic mutations from taking place? For someone like me, that would have prevented my specific disability from developing.

Could there even be a good reason that God allows disabilities and even brings them into our lives for specific reasons? Character can develop through adversity, and an important part of the Christian walk is to become more conformed to the image of Jesus Christ. Therefore, could disabilities be experientially unpleasant yet necessary to develop character and foster spiritual development for certain people in certain times? If so, then even something that we may perceive as less than ideal might be ideal. Disability might be exactly what some people need to bring them to their lives' ultimate purposes. In reflecting on my own life, I am confident that I would not be the person I am today if I had not lived the life I have lived. I'm not claiming to be close to the person I ought to be, but aspects of my character, personality, and attitude have undoubtedly been shaped through the events of my life. Therefore, some could argue my disability exists for my good, even if I don't always feel like it.

Was this world created imperfectly, and therefore bad things happen? This question casts doubt on the goodness of God as Creator or even His position as Creator. If God created imperfectly or if humans are just the product of random chance and blind natural processes, it would not be surprising to find things that are not to our liking. Good would be just as likely to happen as bad, and we would have no justification for expecting to escape evil from either moral or natural causes. An imperfect Creator would be entirely inconsistent with Christian theology, but it is a potential option to avoid the problem of evil. There is no need to solve the problem of evil if there is no expectation that the world began perfectly.[1]

Each question in the previous paragraphs has merit. They are serious, life-framing questions for people who live every day with a variety of disabilities. To understand my place in the world, I need to appraise the situation I find myself in. An important part of who I am is my disability; it is part of my identity. I like to joke that my wheelchair is like an extra body part to me, but that is not really a joke in reality. It is a mechanical extension of who I am, one that I am very sensitive to if people start touching it without my permission.

Similarly, when we talk about the problem of evil, we approach deep questions that touch raw nerves. For some, even suggesting that disability might mean there is something "wrong" with them is offensive. I will attempt to broach this topic charitably but also recognize the reality that there is something wrong with this entire universe because of sin. None of us are as we ought to be, which may manifest itself in many different ways. The consequences of the fall of man are far-reaching.

Consequently, please understand that when I talk about the problem of evil, I am not suggesting in any way that people with disabilities are any more evil than anyone else. I am not suggesting that we are hiding in a lair plotting chaos and destruction. That is not what we mean when we talk about the problem of evil. Instead, when we talk about the problem of evil, we are asking why there are things that are wrong in the world. Apart from those who contend that disability is a social construction and should therefore not be framed as a question of something being "wrong," it seems relatively clear to many that a disability is a condition where something is not working in the way that it is intended to. My muscles do not work in the way that they ought to. For people who are blind, their eyes do not function in the way they were designed to. For people with certain psychological disorders, the chemicals in their bodies are not balanced the way they ought to be. Therefore, when we talk about the problem of evil and something being wrong with disability, please know I am not making any type of moral judgment on people with disabilities (beyond the general fallenness of all mankind due to our sin nature). Rather, I'm trying to understand why disability exists and why things don't always function the way we think they ought to in this world.

---

1   Although my book will not be defending Deism, one might explore Percy Bysshe Shelley, "A Refutation of Deism," in *The Portable Atheist*, ed. Christopher Hitchens (Philadelphia: Da Capo Press, 2007), 50-56, Kindle Edition. This essay provides several arguments from one who found evil an obvious feature of an imperfectly created world.

Approaching this question needs to be done deliberately and cautiously. First and foremost, terms need to be defined. Disability is a complex concept that has been defined in various ways by a variety of different people. Some define disabilities in very explicit categories, while others have a much more open-ended definition of what having a disability means. The first chapter will take on this challenge. The question of why God allows disability falls into the general category of answering the problem of evil. However, there are many different problems of evil, and there are several different types of evil. In response to these problems, three major schools of thought have developed within the Christian community to explain why these various evils exist in the world. The second chapter will attempt to define the problem of evil, and the third chapter will engage with these three Christian approaches to solving the problem of evil and evaluate their relative merits.

The fourth and fifth chapters of this book will help us gain a perspective on the traditional Biblical position regarding disability and how six theologians have responded to the existence of disability. Once all of these pieces are in place, the sixth chapter studies their synthesis and explores how the existence of disability does not disprove the existence of God. The conclusion will provide some final thoughts on this matter and offer a resolution that will comfort Christians trying to reconcile their faith with the reality of disability. Hopefully, it will also challenge nonbelievers who have written off God because they do not believe He could allow disabilities and still be everything Christians say He is.

I have wrestled with my disability and with God. While I have not had any major existential crisis about the purpose of my disability or why I am the way that I am, I have turned this question over in my head many times. I wonder why I have had limitations in my life and why I have received some fantastic opportunities. As I mentioned before, I have been shaped by every element of my life, and having a disability is central to my experience and identity. It is and has always been part of who I am. Therefore, while my academic study of apologetics has not spanned my entire life, this book is the culmination of thoughts that have developed over not just days and weeks but rather years and decades. This work is a combination of lived and academic questioning that I hope will provide you with an intellectual framework to think through these difficult questions that impact so many people daily. I hope it will ultimately bring you hope and answers to some of the world-framing questions that you might find in your life or in the lives of those you love. Complex questions require complex answers rather than simple statements of, "Just have faith." Let us begin to explore together.

Chapter 1

Defining Disability

Disability can be a difficult term to use because it can be defined in various ways. Amy Jacober concurs and says, "We cannot begin to attempt to address all of the variations of disabilities, whether manifested at birth or acquired in life, that include the physical, intellectual, mental, and emotional domains."[1] An individual can acquire a disability at just about any time, and if you live long enough, you are likely to develop a disability at some point in your life. Given that many people can live through conditions that would have been deadly in centuries past, people survive, but they find themselves needing various forms of accommodation to continue functioning in the world. Sometimes that means a ventilator, and sometimes that means a wheelchair. Accommodation can extend to individuals who require different psychological medications and forms of counseling for more hidden disabilities. There is a reason that people call the disability community the largest minority group in the world.[2] As Lamar Hardwick writes, "If you currently leverage any equipment, medication, or other support measures, such as corrective lenses, to assist your body in functioning, then by the broadest definition, you are already a member of the disability community."[3] At some point, almost everyone will find themselves as a member of this community.

Therefore, because disability is such a broad term and can manifest itself in so many different ways, this project cannot just turn to the Oxford English Dictionary, find a definition, and move on. Turning to the appropriate page in that volume yields a definition of, "Lack of ability (to discharge any office or function); inability, incapacity; weakness."[4] While not necessarily wrong, it does

---

1 Amy E. Jacober, *Redefining Perfect: The Interplay Between Theology and Disability* (Eugene, OR: Cascade Books, 2017), chap. 1, Kindle Edition.

2 Judith Heumann and John Wodatch, "We're 20 Percent of America, and We're Still Invisible," *The New York Times,* July 26, 2020, accessed April 20, 2021, https://www.nytimes.com/2020/07/26/opinion/Americans-with-disabilities-act.html.

3 Lamar Hardwick, *Disability and the Church* (Downers Grove, IL: InterVarsity Press, 2021), 12, Kindle Edition.

4 "disability, n," *OED Online,* last modified September 2020, accessed November 26, 2020, https://www.oed.com/view/Entry/53381?redirectedFrom=disability+.

not encompass the entire scope of disability. This definition could just as easily apply to a broken-down car as it could to a human being. This chapter will explore the concept of what disability is and how it should be defined.

The Americans with Disabilities Act (ADA), a life-changing piece of legislation for millions of Americans, provides a solid definition but leaves something to be desired. "An individual with a disability is defined by the ADA as a person who has a physical or mental impairment that substantially limits one or more major life activities, a person who has a history or record of such an impairment, or a person who is perceived by others as having such an impairment."[5] First of all, the ADA definition tightens the focus of what qualifies as a limitation of abilities. A disability needs to interfere with a major life activity. The ADA definition of disability would not consider a sprained thumb a disability because it prevents an athlete from playing basketball. Basketball is important, but it is not a major life activity. Just because you are not blessed with the requisite superhuman endurance does not mean you can claim to have a disability because you cannot climb Mount Everest. The ADA definition assumes that you must be limited in some capacity to have a disability. Not having above-average abilities and being "average" does not qualify as a disability even though you might have less ability than you would like or less ability than some people in the world. The ADA definition remains ambiguous regarding the definition of limitation, but disability is not intended to be applied to everyone. Creating a boundary is an important first step to understanding disability.

Nevertheless, the ADA definition slightly misses the mark regarding its third criterion, which holds that simply the perception of having a disability is equivalent to having a disability. One's disability should not be determined by how someone else perceives them. In my own life, people continually make assumptions about my level of intellect because I use a power wheelchair. Because I have one disability, they assume I have other disabilities along with it. Joni Eareckson Tada was not wrong when she wrote,

> People's hearts will not be changed by the Americans with Disabilities Act, or by health-care reform. People's hearts will not be changed by new legislation, city proclamations, or state declarations. Only the gospel of Jesus Christ can change people's hearts, and the laws and public policies that undergird those laws rest on the hearts of the people.[6]

Even with all the laws in the world, perceptions can still be wrong. As stated in the ADA definition, these inaccurate assumptions are enough to define someone as having a disability because of how the sentence is structured. The potential for

---

5   "A Guide to Disability Rights Laws," *United States Department of Justice, Civil Rights Division*, last modified July 2009, accessed March 5, 2016, http://www.ada.gov/cguide.htm.

6   Joni Eareckson Tada, "Wheelchairs in Heaven?" in *Why, O God?: Suffering and Disability in the Bible and the Church*, eds. Larry J. Waters and Roy B. Zuck (Wheaton: Crossway, 2001), Kindle Edition.

faulty judgments leaves a great deal of ambiguity that makes the ADA definition unsuitable for our purposes.

The United Nations definition of persons with disabilities comes closer to an accurate definition. With a few modifications, it will serve as a reasonable basis to go forward with this investigation of disability and the problem of evil.

> The term persons with disabilities is used to apply to all persons with disabilities including those who have long-term physical, mental, intellectual or sensory impairments which, in interaction with various attitudinal and environmental barriers, hinders their full and effective participation in society on an equal basis with others.[7]

This definition similarly disregards any conversation about duration. For this book, temporary disability is not going to be discussed any further. When society considers what disability is, the popular perception identifies people dealing with long-term physical, mental, intellectual, or sensory impairments. This book is not going to discuss broken wrists or sprained ankles even though they cause temporary limitations.

Despite its initial shortcoming, the United Nations definition states that disabilities are impairments, when combined with other factors, that interfere with full and effective participation in society on an equal basis with others. Their definition is true in a purely natural state, but the United Nations definition allows for the possibility that accommodations can be made to cause an impairment to cease being a disability. For example, an individual who is not able to walk has a disability. Without being able to walk, he or she is not able to fully and effectively participate in society unless there is some adaptive technology such as a wheelchair to facilitate that process. With a wheelchair, this individual will be able to move around, go to work, and do various other things that bring about the equality alluded to at the end of the United Nations definition. The impact of an impairment can be mitigated by adaptive technology, societal acceptance, or other accommodations to help bridge the gap in access.

However, the United Nations definition implies that an individual does not have a disability anymore if he or she can achieve equal access. The separation of disability and impairment is a necessary condition in the United Nations definition of disability because a disability requires a barrier inhibiting the person with an impairment from fully participating in some activity. In contrast, an impairment refers to the medical condition itself. In other words, disability does not refer to a biological reality. Disability is a construct that those in power have built. If the barriers came down and individuals with disabilities could fully participate in society in every way, then disability would cease to exist even if impairment still did.

---

7   "Frequently Asked Questions (FAQs)," *United Nations Enable,* last modified 2007, accessed March 5, 2016, http://www.un.org/esa/socdev/enable/faqs.htm.

The social construction model of disability contains a grain of truth. Societal attitudes and environmental barriers play significant roles in the lives of people with disabilities. There are substantial obstacles that impact everything from employment to housing to recreation to dining. There is no doubt that societal beliefs define what the general population thinks about people with disabilities. They act on those beliefs in ways that do not always positively impact the lives of people with disabilities. Why is the unemployment rate for people with disabilities so high?[8] People make assumptions about capability because of what they have come to believe about people with disabilities. I do not want to claim that societal attitudes and environmental factors have no part to play in the life experiences of people with disabilities. There is an element of disability that is socially constructed.

Nevertheless, I want you to imagine a world where every building has a ramp or an elevator. No one treats me differently because I use my wheelchair, and everyone is perfectly accepting. Amy Jacober provides a problematic conclusion about this kind of world. She quotes, "John Swinton offers a fantastic guiding definition of disability: 'Disability is not defined by any particular impairment or difference. What forms the core of "disability" is the recognition of a shared experience of oppression, marginalization, and injustice.'"[9] Using Swinton's definition of disability as a social construction, I would not have a disability anymore in my imaginary scenario. All of the oppression, marginalization, and injustice would be gone. I would have just as much access as anybody else. There would be nothing impacting my ability to participate in society fully. There would be no attitudinal or physical barriers present in this seemingly amazing world. Everything would be perfectly accommodated for, so there would not be any noticeable difference between the activities I could participate in and the activities that an individual who can walk could enjoy.

The objective fact would be that I would still be unable to walk. I would still need to use my wheelchair. Using the United Nations definition, I would still have an impairment but not a disability. I would still lack a specific ability that other people have. It may not have any impact on my daily life. I could even be followed around by a lifting device that would help me reach the top shelf in every grocery store, so the function of my life would be identical to the function of anyone else's in that instance. Therefore, I would be participating in society on a fully equal basis with everyone else, but the simple fact of the matter is that I would still lack a specific ability. That is the objective fact of the situation in this beautifully perfect, well-accommodated world.

Viewing disability as simply a social construction overlooks basic facts about reality. By considering the biological elements of impairment in its lane

---

8   "Disability Employment Statistics," *United States Department of Labor*, accessed December 28, 2020, https://www.dol.gov/agencies/odep/research/statistics.

9   Amy E. Jacober, *Redefining Perfect: The Interplay Between Theology and Disability* (Eugene, OR: Cascade Books, 2017), chap. 1, Kindle Edition.

separate from the purely social construction of disability, the lives of people with disabilities fall into a kind of dualism. There is not one coherent picture of a whole life. Part of this error is a reaction to the formerly popular medical model of disability that errs on the other side and disregards the impact that external factors can have on the experience of people with disabilities. The medical model internalizes the problems with disability. All of the burden is borne by the individual's biological condition without recognition that accommodation can mitigate issues and obstacles experienced by people with disabilities. As Michael A. Justice points out, "The notion that a church does not need a wheelchair ramp because no one in attendance would use it shows a lack of awareness. The fact that no one attends who uses a wheelchair may be because there are no ramps."[10] Societal attitudes play a role in the lives of those with disabilities. However, the problem inherent in the United Nations definition of disability is that it treats disabilities as a collection of results and activities completed on an equal basis, rather than recognizing the medical reality that still exists despite this functional equality. Segregating medical impairment from socially constructed disability divides the lives of people with disabilities in an unnatural way that is not consistent with the way anyone navigates life. Our lives constantly interact with self and society, and those two interactions should not be separated.

Many are resistant to the medical model because it implies that there is something wrong with an individual with a disability. For instance, Darla Schumm discusses a feminist disability theology that she believes provides a more satisfactory perspective on disability. It emphasizes interdependence rather than charity, which she sees as demeaning. She writes, "A feminist disability ethics of compassion also insists on a rigorous refusal of a charity-based system of care, which reinscribes structures of domination and oppression and which does not work toward true social change and inclusion and justice for all."[11] The clear implication of her theology is that disability is not something to be fixed but rather is a result of a society that needs to change. Admitting our shortcomings flies directly in the face of our postmodern sensibilities as well as our cultural obsession with self-esteem.

Our postmodern sensibilities are offended by acknowledging problems like disability because we refuse to believe that anything can be objectively true. The medical model suggests that disability is a scientific problem that is an objective fact about our medical condition. While there are problems with the assumptions of the medical model and the attitudinal burden it places on individuals with disabilities, as previously stated, the medical model is right about the objective reality that disability is partially a medical problem. Disability is not purely socially constructed.

---

10   Michael A. Justice, "Disabilities and the Church," in *Why, O God?: Suffering and Disability in the Bible and the Church*, eds. Larry J. Waters and Roy B. Zuck (Wheaton: Crossway, 2001), Kindle Edition.

11   Darla Y. Schumm, "Reimaging Disability," *Journal of Feminist Studies in Religion* 26, no. 2 (2010): 136, accessed November 26, 2020, doi:10.2979/fsr.2010.26.2.132.

Our cultural obsession with self-esteem is offended by considering disability a problem. Admitting that disability is a medical problem requires an admission that I may not be perfect just the way I am. Julia Watts Belser and Melanie S. Morrison outright reject the conception that there is anything wrong with disability and explain, "What I wish for us is a way to push back against the ableist assumptions of these healing narratives: that disability is a sign of sin or moral degradation; that we are broken, suffering, and miserable; that we have no agency until our healing comes; that healing is the center of our story and our only longing."[12] The problem with their conception of disability is that healing and reconciliation are the ultimate longings of the human heart. The entire world is broken physically, emotionally, and spiritually. Disability, considered as a problem, is just one more manifestation of the world's brokenness, and the world as a whole is broken. If everything in existence is broken and disability is in existence, then it follows that disability is also evidence of brokenness. Seeking to repair the brokenness and find reconciliation in every aspect of life, including disability, is not demeaning. It is the heart of the Christian doctrine of sin; the world needs reconciliation and cannot find it independently. Once we realize our desperate state, we have the opportunity to respond to the free invitation that God has given us.

Christians believe the entire world is fallen and is broken in a variety of ways. Moral and natural evil cause pain and suffering. For some, the brokenness of the world results in a traumatic accident or a genetic mutation. However, to accept the complete fallenness of the world, we have to admit that we are not perfect either. In a culture where words are often seen as violence[13], it is easy to see why the medical model offends those who cannot admit there is imperfection everywhere.

Again, as mentioned in the introduction, this does not imply that people with disabilities are morally inferior. That would be a terrible misinterpretation of my position. However, the simple fact of the matter is that I have spinal muscular atrophy. A mutation on the fifth chromosome causes my disability. Most people do not have my mutation. My genes are different than other people in a way that causes me to have severe muscle weakness that other people do not have. Some scholars like Deborah Beth Creamer talk about "queering" disability, tearing down barriers, and rejecting divisions. She writes, "The illusion of the ideal body and the distortion of the normal body begin to fade away as we begin to see bodies (or flesh) with new levels of complexity, observing that normal only exists in our imaginations, and recognizing ourselves as having limits and

---

12   Julia Watts Belser and Melanie S. Morrison, "What No Longer Serves Us: Resisting Ableism and Anti-Judaism in New Testament Healing Narratives," *Journal of Feminist Studies in Religion* 27, no. 2 (2011): 163, accessed November 26, 2020, doi:10.2979/jfemistudreli.27.2.153.

13   For more on this cultural development, see Greg Lukianoff and Jonathan Haidt, *The Coddling of the American Mind* (New York: Penguin Press, 2018).

'leaky bodies and boundaries.'"[14] While she does emphasize later in her piece that it is not good to destroy disability identity by disregarding difference, Creamer equates acknowledging the physical reality of disability and the fact that certain bodies are different than others with necessary dehumanization. Acknowledging that someone has a genetic mutation is quite different than classifying a person as subhuman. While some people dehumanize others based on physical, mental, or emotional characteristics, the connection is not logically necessary. It is possible to acknowledge disability, recognize medical conditions that are different from typical, and not dehumanize.

Does SMA make me any less human? Absolutely not, and I am not implying that about any disability. Does that genetic mutation give me a disability? Yes, it does. The problem in my genes gives me a disability. I can't pretend that my genes are perfectly normal and blame society for my disability. While some may seek to divide my impairment as my genetic irregularity and my disability as the socially constructed institutions that deny me full participation in major life activities, the impairment would still exist even if all institutions were perfectly accommodating. I still lack an ability whether or not it functionally inhibits my participation in society. It still is something about me that is chemically different than other people. Human dignity must be maintained while recognizing the diversity in manifestations of the brokenness in the world. Jessica James Baldridge advises, "A person is not defined simply by physical or mental attributes. Every human has some limitations. Churches should accept uniqueness with grace."[15] There is nothing wrong with accepting that humanity has limitations. Church is the one place where we should be open to weakness, no matter how it expresses itself. Hardwick contends, "Unless persons with disabilities have full access to participate fully in all that your church offers, then the church is not functioning as the church should."[16] However, accepting these limitations does not mean denying that limitations exist or pretending that all of us are perfect the way that we are. No one is.

Is disability entirely socially constructed? No, it is not. For the excesses of the medical model and the problems it presents, it does rightly recognize the objective reality that disability is a problem on the individual level. Acknowledging the individuality of disability stands in contrast to disability scholars such as Marcel Broesterhuizen, who suggests, "This shared growing towards the image and likeness of God brings with it a form of Christian perfection which does not have individual perfection as its first goal, but that expresses itself primarily in

---

14   Deborah Beth Creamer, "Embracing Limits, Queering Embodiment: Creating/Creative Possibilities for Disability Theology," *Journal of Feminist Studies in Religion* 26, no. 2 (2010): 125, accessed November 26, 2020, doi:10.2979/fsr.2010.26.2.123.

15   Jessica James Baldridge, "Church-Based Disability Ministries," in *Why, O God?: Suffering and Disability in the Bible and the Church*, eds. Larry J. Waters and Roy B. Zuck (Wheaton: Crossway, 2001), Kindle Edition

16   Lamar Hardwick, *Disability and the Church* (Downers Grove, IL: InterVarsity Press, 2021), 48, Kindle Edition.

the faithfulness and effort with which people build up an inclusive community, in spite of failures and suffering."[17] Many try to separate disability from the individual, and as we will see later in this work, they also try to separate sin from the individual. Disability is experienced on the individual level and to argue that it is entirely socially constructed denies objective reality. Recall the United Nations definition of disability,

> The term persons with disabilities is used to apply to all persons with disabilities including those who have long-term physical, mental, intellectual or sensory impairments which, in interaction with various attitudinal and environmental barriers, hinders their full and effective participation in society on an equal basis with others.[18]

Notice disability necessarily includes a socially constructed element. Impairment, by the United Nations definition, wrongly requires the addition of social factors to qualify as a disability.

Impairment, by the United Nations definition, wrongly requires the addition of social factors to qualify as a disability. Therefore, the definition from the United Nations needs modification even though it is an improvement on the definition of disability used by the ADA.

After looking at both the ADA and United Nations definitions of disability, some common characteristics of disability need to be recognized. First, there is no one-size-fits-all model. There are physical, intellectual, emotional, and sensory impairments, and many disabilities may exhibit features of multiple types of impairments. Secondly, the limitations brought about by various impairments can be exacerbated by attitudinal and environmental barriers. If there is no elevator, it is hard for anyone with limited mobility to access a job opportunity on the fifth floor of a building. Jacober rightly points out that attitudinal barriers are often "the story of many people with disabilities. They are invisible to much of the world. When they are seen, they are too often a problem to solve rather than a person to celebrate."[19] Third, disability can hinder full and effective participation in society or interfere with major life activities unless there is some type of accommodation present. If the accommodation is made, there is no doubt that the disability still exists, but the disability will not necessarily hinder full and effective participation anymore. Despite rejecting the differentiation between disability and impairment, I still recognize that disability has socially constructed elements that can make the degree of disability more or less severe.

---

17   Marcel Broesterhuizen, "A Liberating Approach to Human Contingency," *Gregorianum* 89, no. 1 (2008): 166, accessed November 26, 2020, http://www.jstor.org/stable/23582110.

18   "Frequently Asked Questions (FAQs)," *United Nations Enable,* last modified 2007, accessed March 5, 2016, http://www.un.org/esa/socdev/enable/faqs.htm.

19   Amy E. Jacober, *Redefining Perfect: The Interplay Between Theology and Disability* (Eugene, OR: Cascade Books, 2017), chap. 4, Kindle Edition.

Consequently, for this project, disability is going to be defined as follows: "Disabilities are long-term physical, mental, intellectual or sensory impairments which, in interaction with various attitudinal and environmental barriers, can hinder a person's full and effective participation in society on an equal basis with others or completion of major life activities without appropriate accommodation." This definition seeks to avoid the problems of the medical model, which blames disability on the person with a disability. It also seeks to avoid denying medical reality and arguing that disability is purely a social construct. Instead, disability is an objective medical reality that can be functionally mitigated or exacerbated through interaction with the external world. My motorized wheelchair makes my disability much less disabling than someone who lived centuries ago and could not independently navigate the world.

Disability is difficult to define because there is an entire spectrum of different conditions labeled as disabling. Deborah Kaplan has gone as far as to say,

> The notion that the ADA should only be used to protect persons who are somehow 'truly' disabled reflects an unsophisticated or naive understanding of the nature of disability. Given the significance of social and cultural influences in determining who is regarded as disabled, it makes little sense to refuse to take these same influences into account.[20]

Her statement implies that she would also be critical of the project undertaken in this chapter to provide some boundaries on the term disability.

However, remember that disability is an impairment that exists before the attitudinal and environmental barriers; it is not just a complex of societal perceptions. Disability has an independent existence from the societal barriers that exacerbate the extent of the disability's impact. As a somewhat recent example, in 2015, *The Washington Post* reported that it was possible for Puerto Ricans who could not speak English to qualify for disability benefits in the United States. The rationale behind this decision was that "individuals are considered less employable in the United States if they can't speak English, regardless of their work experience or level of education."[21] The inability to speak English would not qualify as a disability by the definition proposed for this book. Not speaking English is undoubtedly a disadvantage in a country where English is primary. There is nothing about not speaking English that shows any physical, intellectual, emotional. or sensory impairment, though. Disability requires the preexistence of an impairment that does not exist for people who do not speak a particular language.

---

20   Deborah Kaplan, "The Definition of Disability," *The Center for An Accessible Society*, accessed December 28, 2020, http://www.accessiblesociety.org/topics/demographics-identity/dkaplanpaper.htm.

21   Josh Hicks, "Puerto Ricans who can't speak English qualify as disabled for Social Security," *The Washington Post*, April 10, 2015, accessed March 5, 2016, https://www.washingtonpost.com/news/federal-eye/wp/2015/04/10/puerto-ricans-who-cant-speak-english-qualify-as-disabled-for-social-security/.

Joni Eareckson Tada would qualify as a person with a disability in the context of this work. As the founder of the charitable organization Joni and Friends, her story is well known. As a teenager, she had an accident while swimming and ended up with a spinal cord injury. The definition being used for disability throughout this book fits in this situation because her spinal cord injury is, first of all, a long-term condition. Second, it does affect major life activities; Eareckson Tada is a wheelchair user. Attitudinal and environmental barriers affect her life. The extent to which a disability is an obstacle varies from situation to situation due to various factors, but it should at least be clear that in Eareckson Tada's case, it is appropriate to call her medical condition a disability.

Disability is not limited to physical conditions. Down syndrome can have both physical and intellectual effects. Pablo Pineda is a Spanish actor who was the first individual with Down syndrome to graduate from a Spanish university.[22] Pineda is going to have Down syndrome his entire life; it is genetic. Environmental and attitudinal barriers can cause problems for people with all types of disabilities, especially if society does not fully understand an individual's situation. Down syndrome varies widely from person to person, just like any other disability. The extent to which this condition impacts major life activities is incredibly fluid. For some people like Pineda, intellectual ability is impacted very little by Down syndrome; intellectual ability might be much more limited for other people. However, there is very little debate that people with Down syndrome have a disability using this book's definition.

These are just a few examples of disabilities, but the differentiation should be clear. Not everything labeled as a disability by some in society will qualify as a disability by the parameters set in this work. However, by using this definition, the scope of the question can be sufficiently narrowed. At the same time, the diversity of the disability community can be respected. Spinal cord injuries and Down syndrome are dramatically different conditions, but they both belong under the umbrella of disability. The challenges and requisite accommodations necessary for full participation in society will differ, but both qualify as disabilities using this book's definition.

Through this attempt to define disability, it should be clear that disability is complex. Just because you know one person with a disability does not mean that you are now an expert on all disabilities. Even within the community of people with spinal muscular atrophy, the disability can look different for each individual who experiences it. To quote Eareckson Tada again, "I am a quadriplegic. Forty-three years in this wheelchair is a long time. I just celebrated my sixtieth birthday, and I am a weak person. Do not think I am a veteran. I am no professional. I am no

---

22   "Interview: 'Down Syndrome is not a Disease, but Another Personal Characteristic,'" *Disability World*, accessed April 7, 2016, http://www.disabilityworld.org/06-08_03/il/down.shtml.

expert at disability. I need Jesus desperately every single day."[23] It is complicated to establish any specific definition of what a disability is, and I am similarly not going to pretend I alone have come to the perfect answer to this question. I have tried to thoughtfully narrow down this conversation to an approachable and reasonable set of situations that share key characteristics.

A disability must be long-term, it must involve some type of impairment, this impairment must influence the way an individual interacts with the world, and the world can either assist with accommodation or put up further stumbling blocks. These boundaries are still expansive, and there will be some remaining ambiguity. In any such project, counterexamples and exceptions can probably be found. When we discuss the Biblical perspectives on disability in a few chapters, one of the examples we will study, Job, appears to be an exception to the definition laid out because his disability is not long-term. Nevertheless, my proposed definition provides a reasonable basis to consider disability. As our exploration now continues to the problem of evil, this first chapter is foundational for understanding how disability is used in this work.

---

23   Joni Eareckson Tada, "Wheelchairs in Heaven?" in *Why, O God?: Suffering and Disability in the Bible and the Church*, eds. Larry J. Waters and Roy B. Zuck (Wheaton: Crossway, 2001), Kindle Edition.

Chapter 2

Defining the Problem of Evil

The problem of evil is the most substantial challenge leveled at the Christian faith. For millennia, people have considered why God allows evil to remain or why it even exists in the first place. Job was most likely the first book of the Bible written, and its central theme concerns the role of suffering and evil. In the book of Psalms, there are many instances where David speaks about problems he faces and asks why God allows evil in his life. The Gospels present an image of a perfect Savior who takes on the sin of the world. He suffers great evil at the hands of men to bring salvation to humanity. The apostle Paul was no stranger to evil in his own life, and he wrote a great deal about suffering through his epistles. John wrote about the end of evil in Revelation. The Bible addresses evil almost cover to cover because humanity continually wrestles with its existence. There is no doubt that the problem of evil has been among the central challenges to the Christian faith from its inception.

Experientially, even the most devout Christians have struggled with dark times. Many people know what it is like to wonder where God is when a loved one dies or a business goes bankrupt. These very real storms feel wrong. It is one thing to read about David experiencing evil in his life. That was what he had to go through, and it is simple for me to say that God had a purpose for all of David's suffering. After all, we know the end of the story, and we have rationally considered David's situation. God used the adversity in David's life to do great things, so it is easier to see why he went through the trials he did.

It feels entirely different when I need to face suffering in my life. Logically, there is no reason that I should expect any more or less suffering than David; we are both men living in a fallen world many years apart. God could be using my situation much like He used David's. Providence still exists today. Therefore, I should be no more concerned about my situation than I am about David's. My emotions tell me a different story. The logic I know does not necessarily quiet my emotions during whatever storm I find myself in.

This simple differentiation between how I feel about evil in general and how I feel about evil in my own life illustrates the two questions underlying the problem of evil. On the one hand, there is the philosophical problem of evil, and on the other hand, there is the experiential problem of evil. Other subproblems within these larger problems will be discussed briefly, but it is critical to remember that there are two main problems of evil; one is logical while one is more emotional.

David Hume provided an early, clear outline of the philosophical problem of evil. Hume presented the problem of evil in this way, "Epicurus's old questions are yet unanswered. Is he willing to prevent evil, but not able? Then is he impotent. Is he able, but not willing? Then is he malevolent. Is he both able and willing? Whence then is evil?"[1] There are a few crucial features to Hume's argument. The first question is why evil exists, and Hume asks if God is not powerful enough to remove evil. For Christians, this is problematic because it calls into question the omnipotence of God. Hume then proposes a second option. Maybe God does have the power to eliminate evil, but He simply does not want to. Hume suggests this would make God malevolent. Assuming a malevolent God is problematic for Christians who believe in a God who is love. A malevolent God would not allow evil just to bring about a greater good; He would be cruel and let evil happen. For Hume, it is unreasonable to assume that God might allow evil for soul-making or closer conformance to the image of Jesus Christ. It would make more sense to bring about the greater good without evil, given that God is all-powerful and assuming that He wants what is good for humanity. If God is powerful enough to eliminate evil and wants to eliminate evil, Hume then questions why evil exists. He can only conclude that God must be malevolent.

Hume's argument was developed further by J. L. Mackie. Mackie recognized, like Hume, that God's omnipotence and omnibenevolence were critical. He wrote, "In its simplest form, the problem is this: God is omnipotent; God is wholly good; and yet evil exists. There seems to be some contradiction between these three propositions, so that if any two of them were true the third would be false."[2] Mackie formalized the problem of evil by supposing there is a logical inconsistency between his three propositions. The problem of evil is not simply a question of why there is evil as in Hume's formulation. While Hume presented a rhetorical question that he assumed could not be answered, it strikes a different tone than Mackie's proposition. Mackie suggests an absolute logical impossibility in that two of these premises cannot be true without the third one being false. The problem of evil is no longer a question; it is a fact.

Mackie's basic argument, however, is too simple. Evil does not only come in one variety. Talking about the problem of evil that arises from a personal choice is much different than asking why God brings a hurricane. Moral evil is the most widely discussed form of evil. Jeremy A. Evans defined this kind of evil as "when free persons misuse their freedom in such a way that the content of their will and/or actions violates a moral standard."[3] From a Christian worldview, God has

---

1   David Hume, *Dialogues Concerning Natural Religion*, ed. Richard H Popkin (Indianapolis: Hackett Publishing Company, 1998), 63, Kindle Edition.

2   J. L. Mackie, "Evil and Omnipotence," *Mind* 64, No. 254 (April 1955): 200, accessed March 5, 2016, http://www.jstor.org/stable/2251467.

3   Jeremy A. Evans, *The Problem of Evil: The Challenge to Essential Christian Beliefs* (Nashville: B&H Academic, 2013), 2, Kindle Edition.

outlined the moral standards of right and wrong. These flow out of His character. Therefore, when people violate God's standards, they have committed moral evil. Moral evil includes the obvious sins of murder, envy, theft, and dishonesty but also so many others. It can involve crimes committed against one person or millions. Moral evil carries a different meaning for different people occasionally. Some might say that every single lie is a moral evil, while others might say that there are times when it is morally permissible to lie. The definition of moral evil is not universally agreed upon, but it serves as a classification term in this work. Moral evil is the sin that people commit and is typically what people refer to when they speak about evil.

Sometimes the earth itself seems to be evil. Tsunamis devastate villages in Asia, and tornadoes decimate towns in the Midwest United States. These are examples of natural evil; Evans identifies it as the evil that arises from nonhuman sources yet still causes suffering for humans.[4] Some would argue that human activity does affect the natural world, and therefore natural evil is related to moral evil. Some people might say, for example, that global warming brings about changes in weather patterns that create a longer hurricane season, and the same people might argue that global warming is primarily a human creation. Therefore, they would probably classify the overlap in human action and natural effect as moral evil transforming into natural evil. However, natural evil is understood as something separate from moral evil and beyond human control in most cases.

Because purely natural evil is mainly beyond the control of any individual, one must consider God's role in natural evil. It is easy to blame moral evil on human free will. As free agents, individuals commit wrong actions that harm themselves and others. Therefore, one could argue that the choices of free agents do not impact the goodness of God. This response will be examined in greater detail later in this book, but for the time being, it is important to note that this defense seems insufficient for considering natural evil. A different type of perceived evil is going to require a different answer.

With moral and natural evil in mind, Peter van Inwagen outlines multiple ways to understand what the problem is with evil. There are practical problems of evil that focus on personal and pastoral issues. There are also theoretical problems of evil that focus on doctrinal and apologetic dilemmas.[5] Both moral and natural evil can apply to each of these four types of problems.

The personal problem of evil is the most specific. Van Inwagen writes,

A personal problem arises typically when one, or someone whom one is close to, suffers some terrible misfortune; or, less typically, when one suddenly

---

4 Jeremy A. Evans, *The Problem of Evil: The Challenge to Essential Christian Beliefs* (Nashville: B&H Academic, 2013), 4, Kindle Edition.

5 Peter van Inwagen, *The Problem of Evil* (New York: Oxford University Press, 2006), Lecture 1, Kindle Edition.

learns of some terrible event in the public sphere that does not directly affect one but nevertheless engages one's general human sympathies.[6]

Disability primarily relates to the problem of evil through the personal problem of evil combined with the problem of natural evil. The personal problem of evil is the problem that comes into play when a child is born with a genetic disorder. It is the problem that becomes evident when an individual experiences a traumatic event that has a psychological impact for years. One specific person is facing a difficult circumstance. The personal problem of evil is the basic level of evil that most directly impacts most people most of the time.

The pastoral problem of evil considers how to help people suffering from the personal problem of evil. According to van Inwagen, "Pastoral problems of evil raise the question: What spiritual guidance shall I give to someone for whom some terrible thing has raised practical questions about his relationship with God?"[7] The pastoral problem of evil directly impacts the lives of those who have disabilities every day. How can people best support their friends who are living with disabilities? The pastoral problem of evil faces a girlfriend when she visits her boyfriend in a rehabilitation hospital while he recovers from a spinal cord injury. She wants to know how she can help him, but she might not know how to adjust to their new reality as a couple. The pastoral problem of evil challenges parents as they try to make choices to help their child thrive. They want to know how to best care for and support this young life that has been entrusted to their care. In both situations, the pastoral problem of evil raises questions of love and how best to come alongside people who are experiencing life with a disability.

The pastoral problem of evil is also at the heart of all disability accommodation. Even though the chief concern of this book is the spiritual issue of evil, the pastoral problem of evil incorporates many of the societal issues that disability rights advocates point to when they discuss disability being a social construction. Providing spiritual support often means providing tangible, physical, or emotional support as well. There is a connection between spiritual health and community inclusion.[8] The pastoral problem of evil is answered when considering how to best support those who need ramps or American Sign Language interpretation. Combating the pastoral problem of evil can be a way of demonstrating love for those around us with and without disabilities.

Although the pastoral problem of evil will not be the central theme of this book, it is important to recognize that these pastoral concerns affect the families and friends of those with disabilities too. It is not only the person with a disability who needs support from others. Families, particularly parents, have

---

6   Peter van Inwagen, *The Problem of Evil* (New York: Oxford University Press, 2006), Lecture 1, Kindle Edition

7   Ibid.

8   This relationship is a major theme in Lamar Hardwick, *Disability and the Church* (Downers Grove, IL: InterVarsity Press, 2021).

many questions about why these difficult circumstances have arisen in their lives and the lives of their loved ones. Therefore, it is wise to consider how to provide comfort and encouragement both to people with disabilities and those who love them. Family members tend to be overlooked by disability ministries.

The first theoretical problem of evil is the doctrinal problem. Van Inwagen explains, "Doctrinal problems are problems that are created by the fact that almost all theists subscribe to some well-worked-out and comprehensive theology that goes far beyond the assertion of the existence of an all-powerful and beneficent Creator."[9] The doctrinal problem of evil is what Hume and Mackie attack. They understand Christians have certain beliefs about the nature of God. Christians consider God to be omnipotent, omniscient, and omnibenevolent. However, they point out that this combination of characteristics seems logically inconsistent with the existence of evil. They hold that it is not possible for God to be morally perfect, all-knowing, and all-powerful and simultaneously allow for the existence of evil. The problem of evil is only a problem because of the type of God that Christians claim God is.

The doctrinal problem of evil is not a problem for all religions because not all religions believe that God or the gods have the same attributes. Specifically, if a religion does not believe its deities are omnipotent, omniscient, and omnibenevolent, the problem of evil disappears. Perhaps this is why there is a great deal of interest in being spiritual but not religious.[10] The higher power of the spiritual but not religious does not need to have any specific characteristics. They can enjoy all of the benefits of believing in a higher power without committing to the specifics that need to reconcile with the existence of evil. While Christians have to wrestle with reconciling their omnipotent, omniscient, and omnibenevolent God with the existence of evil, the spiritual but not religious do not have to do that because their frequently self-defined higher power does not need to have all three of those characteristics. If an unnamed, amorphous higher power is good but can't stop evil, the problem of evil does not exist. If that higher power is essentially a super powered human, with all power and ability but a questionable moral code at times, then the problem of evil is not a problem. The doctrinal problem of evil is a problem for orthodox Christians, but it would not apply to any belief system where their higher power is not omnipotent, omniscient, and omnibenevolent.

Finally, the apologetic problem of evil is similar to the pastoral problem in that it attempts to communicate and discuss the problem of evil with particularly nonbelievers. Van Inwagen explains, "The apologetic problem is, in fact, the problem of what to say in response to the argument from evil. It is, at any rate, that problem as it confronts those who, for one reason or another, regard

---

9   Peter van Inwagen, *The Problem of Evil* (New York: Oxford University Press, 2006), Lecture 1, Kindle Edition.

10   "Meet the 'Spiritual but Not Religious'," *Barna*, April 6, 2017, accessed December 28, 2020, https://www.barna.com/research/meet-spiritual-not-religious/.

themselves as responsible for the defense of theism or of Christianity or of some other theistic religion."[11] Answering objections is what Christians are called to do. It is the mission of apologists but should be the mission of all Christians. This entire book is meant to take the problem of evil as it relates to disability and translate it into terms that make sense in the face of sometimes highly emotional and troubling circumstances. While many will believe in God and understand that the problem of evil does not disprove the existence of God, the apologist needs to be able to relate both truths to people who see their simultaneous existence as a problem. It is necessary to defend Christian theism against the charge that the existence of disability somehow proves that God is not omnipotent, omniscient, and omnibenevolent.

Some will argue that the charge of the irrationality of Christianity does not need to be answered. All you need to do is have faith in God. Nothing else matters. The leap of faith is called fideism and is best understood as having entirely blind faith, not based on any rational understanding of the doctrine of God. Attempting to delve into the inner workings of God is at best a fool's errand and is at worst demonstrating a lack of true faith. The fideist would contend that apologetic problems should not be answered because true faith does not require reason. Fideism erroneously bypasses the problem of evil by ignoring the entire field of apologetics and denying its relevance.

In response to the fideists' charge, it is important to remember people like Hume and Mackie. They believe that they have reason on their side and have, therefore, entirely written off the truth of the Christian worldview and the reality of the Christian God. What shall we say to them if the only thing we can tell them is to have more faith? Are we abandoning them for lost?

Would it not be more effective to engage them on their terrain? God is indeed a God of truth. As a result, Christians ought not be afraid to follow truth wherever it leads, and that includes delving into the realm of philosophy. The balance of this book will seek to engage the problem of evil philosophically. There are philosophical options for the Christian to answer the problem of evil. Not everyone will require those reasons, but people who want to build a strong foundation for their faith will. Therefore, if Christians are genuinely committed to the Great Commission and want to spread the gospel to the entire world, our mission must include those who need these kinds of evidence. The apologetic problem of evil exists because Christians should believe people with deep-seated questions should not be forgotten.

Understanding the different problems of evil and moral and natural evil will provide a basis to advance our argument further. Naturally, different problems and different types of evil require different responses. For example, there are times when a pastoral response will be best. Sometimes, people need words of comfort when facing difficult circumstances, and it might not necessarily be the

---

11   Peter van Inwagen, *The Problem of Evil* (New York: Oxford University Press, 2006), Lecture 1, Kindle Edition.

best time to dive into a discussion of the doctrinal problem of evil. Even if it might be true that someone's abuse of free will caused an injury that resulted in a disability, an explanation of why God had to allow that action to take place rather than impinge on human free will is not always appropriate. Evil manifests itself in various forms, and it needs to be addressed in a way that is appropriate for its form. It is not that doctrine cannot be comforting, but there are situations where people just want to be listened to and sympathized with, like when Jesus wept with the family of Lazarus.[12] He could have immediately started preaching doctrine, and it would not have been morally wrong to speak doctrinal truths. However, Jesus chose the more effective way by simply being there and loving His friends. He understood that there are multiple levels to the problem of evil, and the correct response depends on the situation. Truth must not be compromised, but empathy sometimes requires listening rather than preaching.

The problem of evil has existed since evil entered the world. There are two primary classes of evil: moral and natural. Four main problems of evil stem from these classes of evil: personal, pastoral, doctrinal, and apologetic. All of these elements can interact with each other, but the problem of evil essentially boils down to the question of how God, if He is everything orthodox Christians say He is, can allow so much moral and natural evil in the world which causes so many personal, pastoral, doctrinal, and apologetic problems? The remainder of this book will seek to address this question.

---

12   John 11:35, ESV.

Chapter 3

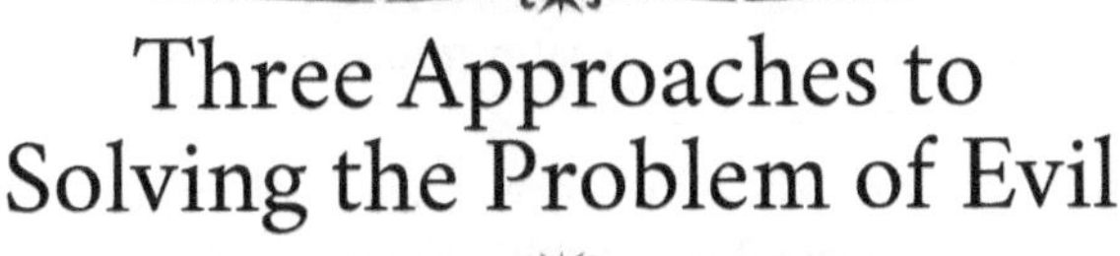

Three Approaches to Solving the Problem of Evil

Three primary schools of thought have prevailed as the most popular Christian options for responding to the problem of evil. The first is commonly referred to as the free will defense, and Alvin Plantinga most famously champions it. In its simple form, this approach contends God gave humanity free will, which is a great good. However, that great good was abused by humans, and, as a result, the world still suffers from the consequences of evil decisions. The second general approach is referred to as a soul-making theodicy. Richard Swinburne has defended it, and, in its simple form, it suggests God allows evil in the world because it creates good in people. As an example, the virtue of courage would never develop if nothing was frightening. Therefore, it is not problematic that people view some things as evil in the world. These seemingly bad events are part of the plan God has put together. Lastly, the Reformed perspective suggests that since God determines what will happen and how the story of history will play out, evil is the tension that creates the drama and the beauty of the story and displays God's goodness and justice.

In the following sections, each of these perspectives will be presented more fully. Each model has strengths and weaknesses. Therefore, by viewing each of those approaches critically, it is possible to begin discussing the ultimate question of this book. How does one address the problem of evil in the light of disability?

A. The Free Will Defense

As presented by Plantinga, the problem of evil includes two implicit premises that remain unstated in most formulations.

The two additional principles [the atheologian] suggests are (19) A good thing always eliminates evil as far as it can and (20) There are no limits to what an omnipotent being can do. And, of course, if Mackie means to show that set A is implicitly contradictory, then he must hold that (19) and (20) are not merely true but necessarily true.[1]

---

1   Alvin Plantinga, *God, Freedom, and Evil* (Grand Rapids: Wm. B. Eerdmans, 1977), pt. I.a.1, Kindle Edition.

These two additional premises provide the opportunity Plantinga uses to speak about the good of free will. Standing particularly on the first premise, the atheologian claims that there is no logical reason God could have for allowing evil. In other words, there is no possible greater good that God could give humanity that would justify the existence of evil.

Plantinga suggests that there are times when there are two bad choices, but people are forced to decide. "It is entirely possible that a good person fail to eliminate an evil state of affairs that he knows about and can eliminate. This would take place, if, as in the present example, he couldn't eliminate the evil without bringing about a greater evil."[2] Plantinga's assertion seems to be practically and experientially true. A common expression of choosing the lesser of two evils occurs when the railroad conductor has to decide which train track to send a runaway train down. There will be damage and lives lost in either case, but no one would call the conductor evil for having to choose between two states that are not ideal. Because of the conductor's moral permissibility in choosing the lesser of two evils, Plantinga reformulates the first additional premise to make the problem of evil an actual problem. "A good being eliminates every evil E that it knows about and that it can eliminate without either bringing about a greater evil or eliminating a good state of affairs that outweighs E."[3] Modifying the premise removes the opportunity for the free will defender to stop the problem of evil by simply appealing to the lesser of two evils.

Plantinga then advances the argument that perhaps the good state of affairs that outweighs the amount of evil in the world is the existence of human free will.

> The Free Will Defense can be looked upon as an effort to show that there may be a very different kind of good that God can't bring about without permitting evil. These are good states of affairs that don't include evil; they do not entail the existence of any evil whatever; nonetheless God Himself can't bring them about without permitting evil.[4]

In his defense, Plantinga makes a strong assumption and writes, "A world containing creatures who are significantly free (and freely perform more good than evil actions) is more valuable, all else being equal, than a world containing no free creatures at all."[5] Critics will challenge that freedom is not a sufficient justification for allowing the potential of evil. God could have created robots. God could have created only people who would perfectly follow His law. If God had done so, then the problem of evil would not exist. Everyone would follow God perfectly, and Paradise would never have been lost. Would the hypothetical Paradise that would have existed for robot Adam and robot Eve have been Paradise, though?

---

2   Alvin Plantinga, *God, Freedom, and Evil* (Grand Rapids: Wm. B. Eerdmans, 1977), pt. I.a.2, Kindle Edition.

3   Ibid.

4   Ibid., pt. I.a.4.

5   Ibid.

Robots are not capable of developing a relationship with God. They would be preprogrammed, so it would be impossible for them to do anything against the will of their Maker. They would not be able to do evil, but they would also not be able to do anything good. They would not be responsible for any of their actions; the potential for doing good necessarily entails the potential for doing evil. Plantinga writes,

> The heart of the Free Will Defense is the claim that it is possible that God could not have created a universe containing moral good (or as much moral good as this world contains) without creating one that also contained moral evil. And if so, then it is possible that God has a good reason for creating a world containing evil.[6]

Just like there cannot be darkness without light, there cannot be the choice to do good without the choice to do evil. A good action done without the choice to do evil might not even be actually good.

Consider the difference between doing something out of obligation and doing something out of love. A waiter brings food to a table because it is his job, and he receives wages. A mother brings food to the table because she loves her children; there is no compensation for her service. It is not that the waiter is doing anything wrong. Delivering food is simply an obligation that he has to honor based on the money that diners have spent to buy a service. He does not have to love any of the patrons to be a good waiter. He can fulfill his obligation to provide excellent service without any deeper commitment without impinging the moral goodness of fulfilling his obligation. Waiting tables is an almost robotic service that does not require intimacy.

A mother, on the other hand, is doing something morally good when she loves. One can argue that a mother has an obligation to her children, similar to a waiter. However, it is not as if a mother is receiving compensation for providing a service for her children. She is doing it because it is the right thing to do. However, that sense of obligation goes beyond the almost robotic service of a waiter. If a mother does not love her children, we would question her moral goodness because of the ideal relationship between a parent and child. Without love, one could argue that even when a mother brings food to the table, if she does it without love, she is not fulfilling her duty as a mother to love her family.

Because of the difference between obligation and love, it is easy to see why Plantinga would believe that a world capable of moral good is better than a world without that possibility; it allows for love and relationship. To perform actions that are morally good and require love and relationship, people need to be free. They need to be able to choose to care for their fellow human beings. Because a mother has to go beyond the arguably robotic obligation to deliver food to her children to the level of love to be considered morally good, there is a chance that a mother will not go beyond that level and therefore fall into moral failure. Parents

---

6   Alvin Plantinga, *God, Freedom, and Evil* (Grand Rapids: Wm. B. Eerdmans, 1977), pt. I.a.4, Kindle Edition.

can provide for their children, fulfilling that obligation like a waiter, but fail to show their children any love, thus failing to demonstrate moral goodness.

One might wonder then why risk love or relationship at all? Why risk failure? The answer is that freedom and the choice to do good is enough of a moral good to offset the risk of failure. Inherent in that freedom to choose is a risk of abuse. Wrong choices bring about evil in the world, but despite all the evil in the world, it is not enough evil to justify restricting the goodness of human freedom.

As simple as this explanation seems to be, there is a substantial challenge to be made to the central contention of the free will defense. If God can create any possible world and if it is possible for a person to always make the right decision, why did God decide to make the world that currently exists? Plantinga draws on Leibniz to argue that God created the best possible world He was able to. "While Leibniz draws the conclusion that this world, despite appearances, must be the best possible, Mackie concludes instead that there is no omnipotent, wholly good God. For, he says, it is obvious enough that this present world is not the best of all possible worlds."[7] Plantinga's response lies in a concept called transworld depravity. His discussion gets slightly technical in this portion:

> Now God can create a world containing moral good only by creating significantly free persons. And, since every person is the instantiation of an essence, He can create significantly free persons only by instantiating some essences. But if every essence suffers from transworld depravity, then no matter which essences God instantiates, the resulting persons, if free with respect to morally significant actions, would always perform at least some wrong actions. If every essence suffers from transworld depravity, then it was beyond the power of God Himself to create a world containing moral good but no moral evil. He might have been able to create worlds in which moral evil is very considerably outweighed by moral good; but it was not within His power to create worlds containing moral good but no moral evil — and this despite the fact that He is omnipotent. Under these conditions God could have created a world containing no moral evil only by creating one without significantly free persons. But it is possible that every essence suffers from transworld depravity; so it's possible that God could not have created a world containing moral good but no moral evil.[8]

Outside of Jesus Christ, there has never been a perfect person. Everyone makes plenty of wrong decisions every day, if not every hour or minute. Therefore, because humans seem to have this propensity to do wrong things, it is no surprise that people would still hurt themselves or other people in any possible world. It is a sad fact of existence, but it seems like, given free choice, people will still make wrong decisions now and then. No one is perfect.

---

7   Alvin Plantinga, *God, Freedom, and Evil* (Grand Rapids: Wm. B. Eerdmans, 1977), pt. I.a.4, Kindle Edition.

8   Ibid., pt. I.a.7.

Nevertheless, the assumption of transworld depravity is the biggest problem with the free will defense. Because people only have experience in the current world, how is it possible to assume that there would still be depravity in any possible world? It could be argued that in the Garden of Eden, Adam and Eve lived some undefined time without making any sinful decisions. The Bible does not define how long they existed there before the fall, but there was a period where they lived in accordance with the will of God. Had they never fallen for the deception of the serpent, they could have lived longer in the Garden without falling away from God. There is no doubt that there was a time when people made all of the right choices.

If it was possible in the short-term, then it seems that it could be possible in the long-term as well. If God created Adam and Eve, who could freely make the right decisions for at least some amount of time, then transworld depravity seems to be in a bit of a difficult situation. Adam and Eve did not necessarily have to sin, even though they eventually did. Of course, that might be the rebuttal from Plantinga. The very fact that they fell is evidence that even in a perfect world, humans still ultimately make wrong decisions.

Plantinga, it should be noted, acknowledges that it is possible God could have created a world with no moral evil and allow free choice. That means that it is possible that God could have created a world with no moral evil permanently and still allow for moral good. Plantinga is not saying that He definitely could have, but he stopped short of saying that it was impossible. Suggesting there might be a possible world where freely made choices are always right may seem to undercut the entire argument of transworld depravity. What Plantinga says in response, however, is consistent with human experience. Individuals with free will will always make wrong choices eventually because it is in their essence to do so. Human history seems to provide very good evidence for this conclusion without any morally perfect counterexample outside of Jesus Christ. Assuming free beings will always make wrong choices eventually is also consistent with Christian theology which claims that all have sinned.

Another advocate of the free will defense, David Bentley Hart, has an alternative way of handling the necessity of man's fallenness. He writes, "As God did not will the fall, and yet always wills all things toward ward himself, the entire history of sin and death is in an ultimate sense a pure contingency, one that is not as such desired by God, but that is nevertheless constrained by providence to serve his transcendent purpose."[9] Rather than speaking about possible worlds and wondering why God might not have created a more perfect world, Hart prefers to stay in the reality of the world that God created. He believes that God created the world perfectly, but sin has twisted things that were initially good. Hart explains, "It is impossible to desire anything without implicitly desiring the infinite source of all things; even the desire of the suicide for the peace of oblivion is born of a love of self — however tragically distorted it has become — that is

---

9   David Bentley Hart, *The Doors of the Sea: Where Was God in the Tsunami?* (Grand Rapids: Wm. B. Eerdmans, 2005), chap. 2, pt.4, Kindle Edition.

itself born of a deeper love for the God from whom the self comes and to whom the self is called."[10]

If free will is truly good, which both Plantinga and Hart would affirm, God would not be responsible for the abuse of that good gift. Even if free will has been used in morally wrong ways, because of the nature of freedom, the agents who made those choices would be responsible for their own decisions. Hart continues, "God has fashioned creatures in his image so that they might be joined in a perfect union with him in the rational freedom of love. For that very reason, what God permits, rather than violate the autonomy of the created world, may be in itself contrary to what he wills."[11] Imagine a father allowing his son the freedom to go out with his friends on a Friday night. The child might not do everything that his parent would want him to. The son might make some decisions that are entirely contrary to what his father would want. However, if this boy does anything wrong, his father would not be morally responsible for his son's choices. Freedom necessarily involves risk, but that does not mean that the one who gives the freedom is responsible for the abuses of that freedom. Continuing the same argument, it is a good thing for parents to give freedom to their children. At some point, individuals need to act as individuals and make their own decisions. It would not be a good thing if children never developed any independence. The world is more valuable when children can choose and when there are more independent, free beings in the world. Beings with more freedom create a better situation than comparatively less free beings. It is a good thing for children on earth to eventually gain freedom, and in the same way, it is a good thing for God to grant His children freedom.

The difference between allowing and creating evil is the most crucial concept behind any formulation of the free will defense. God is not responsible for evil; in fact, this is the charge that seems to move many defenders of the free will defense to this perspective in the first place. God gave His children a gift that is truly very good. Freedom is better than no freedom. God did not create robots, but He created people who are capable of making decisions. Freedom is a good thing, but because freedom is unrestricted, people are free to reject God if they decide to. Rejecting God leads to a variety of dire consequences. If God is good, then rejecting that which is good is going to bring about evil. As a result, evil is not God's responsibility. Evil is not something that God created. Instead, freedom, a good gift, is abused by people who make free decisions to embrace the idolatry of the self. They decide that they want to be like God, and, in doing so, they reject God.

For the defender of the free will defense, free will is a very great good, but it was abused by humanity. Having freedom and potentially abusing it is a greater good than not having freedom and being a robot. Because of the implicit premise

---

10   David Bentley Hart, *The Doors of the Sea: Where Was God in the Tsunami?* (Grand Rapids: Wm. B. Eerdmans, 2005), chap. 2, pt.4, Kindle Edition.

11   Ibid.

that God can allow for the possibility of humanly-chosen evil if there is a greater good to be had, the free will defense solves the logical problem of evil. If free will is such a great good that its existence provides a better world than one without evil and free choice, then the logical problem of evil is not a problem. For the Christian, if having a relationship with God, only possible through free choice rather than through robotic obligation, is better than a world without the possibility of a relationship with God, then the logical problem of evil is solved.

Solving the logical problem of evil does not directly resolve the emotional problem of evil. For some people, intellectual solutions will be comforting, but some people need more than intellectual assent. Outlining the free will defense does not seem to be the most effective pastoral approach to take to the problem of evil. However, what the free will defense does is help address one part of the problem. It shows why the Christian does not have to logically write off the existence of God because of evil in the world. It does not mean that it is easy to process the existence of evil emotionally, but it does mean that it is quite possible for there to be a reason that God has allowed evil and suffering in the world.

B. The Soul-Making Theodicy

It is not uncommon to hear people speak about improving their character while going through difficult times. Courage, for instance, cannot be learned outside of facing fears. Bilbo Baggins would have remained a gentle-hobbit with no appetite for adventures if he did not face challenges that forced him to grow. Forgiveness cannot be learned unless there has been an offense that requires being forgiven. The testimony of missionary Elisabeth Elliot would not be nearly as powerful if she had not learned to embrace forgiveness after her husband was murdered by the tribe he was trying to minister to in Ecuador. Because these are good characteristics, it seems to be the case that the world is a better place when they are developed.

Assuming that adversity develops character is the foundation of any type of soul-making theodicy. Swinburne argues that God has the right to bring about any affairs He chooses to. "Since one is obliged not to do that which one does not have the right to do and God always fulfils his obligations, the bad states which he allows to occur must be ones which he has the right to allow to occur."[12] The Christian God is described in a particular fashion through the pages of the Bible. Among these characteristics is the fact that God is just. Therefore, if God is just, He is not going to do anything unjust. God has a right to allow whatever bad states He wants and is still just. Swinburne continues, "It is not always a bad act to bring about or to allow to occur a bad state of affairs."[13] Just as the free will defender argues that it is justifiable for God to allow the risk of the abuse of free

---

12   Richard Swinburne, *Providence and the Problem of Evil* (New York: Oxford University Press, 1998), 22, Kindle Edition.

13   Ibid., 21.

will for the greater good of allowing human choice, Swinburne argues God can justify allowing certain bad states to occur. He uses a comparison to dental work to illustrate his point. "Thus the only way in which a human parent can get his child's teeth repaired may be by taking him to the dentist and allowing pain to be inflicted upon him; and sometimes the only way in which he can reform the child may be to punish him by deliberately inflicting suffering upon him."[14] Suffering is not always a bad thing, even though it may not be pleasant at the time. Suffering can lead to a greater good.

As an example of something good, Swinburne talks about the idea of belief. A true belief is a good thing. "A true belief about which road leads home will enable me to bring about the fulfilment of my desire to be at home."[15] Having a belief that corresponds to the way reality truly behaves is ultimately good. Therefore, a false belief is something that is not good. If someone holds a belief that does not correspond with reality, no one will benefit. To further the example from the previous paragraph, telling someone that they have an incorrect belief will not be pleasant. They will not be happy that you are contradicting them and pushing them toward reality. However, that intervention is necessary to bring about a state of greater good, more people believing a true belief instead of a falsehood.

Similarly, if one has a desire, it can be good or bad. Some things are good to seek after, while others are bad. Rejecting a bad desire may not feel good. Some bad desires are very tempting and alluring, and it takes all our strength to fight them. However, experiencing deprivation avoids the negative consequences of bad desires. Therefore, the future is made better because of pain in the present. Getting to the better state has consequences, but they are worth it if the end is sufficiently good.

Swinburne also embraces free will, although he differentiates his position from Plantinga's by rejecting God's eternal omniscience. "If God gives us freedom to choose between right and wrong, he cannot foreknow incorrigibly how we will choose; and so he inevitably allows the possibility of our doing wrong."[16] Swinburne comes into conflict with Plantinga's transworld depravity. Transworld depravity presupposes that there is no possible way that the essence of created people could be put in a perfect world where they always make perfect decisions. In other words, even though there is much evil in this world, it is the best possible world that could be created. Plantinga would argue that God indeed knows that and chose the best possible outcome, whereas Swinburne would say that God cannot possibly know the best possible outcome. God is omniscient, but that omniscience does not extend to the choices of free agents. He argues that for free will to truly be free, it cannot be predetermined or foreknown in any fashion.

---

14   Richard Swinburne, *Providence and the Problem of Evil* (New York: Oxford University Press, 1998), 21, Kindle Edition.

15   Ibid., 66.

16   Ibid., 144.

Swinburne naturally then needs a different explanation for why God allows evil. If Plantinga argued that God allowed people to have free will and the resulting world is the best possible world, it makes sense that even though there might be some evil, God had to take that trade-off if He would allow for free will. God is working through bad circumstances providentially to create the best world possible. On the other hand, Swinburne argues that God does not have divine foreknowledge, so it would be impossible to determine that this is the best possible world. Swinburne recognizes that this type of world allows the possibility of a great deal of moral evil.

> It is no doubt good to stop others acting hastily under the influence of a desire which they desire or think it good not to have; but bad to stop someone exercising an ultimate freedom whose consequences he desires, and desires to desire, and has thought through. But once again in all these ways much responsibility given to free agents will make it enormously probable that there will be much moral evil unprevented by God.[17]

Swinburne's conception sounds like an incredibly risky proposition for God. After all, God would be walking into the future blind. By giving humans libertarian free will, God gives up control over what happens. However, Swinburne points out that for every bad state that God potentially allows, there is a greater good, the creation of better souls in humans:

> Every moral evil in the world is such that God allowing it to occur makes possible (given the assumption that humans have free will) the great good of a particular choice between good and bad. Every bad desire facilitates such a choice. Every false belief makes possible the great good of investigation, especially cooperative investigation, and the great good of some of us helping others towards the truth. Every pain makes possible a courageous response (in all except animals caused to respond badly, and humans who do not yet realize what is the good response), and normally the goods of compassion and sympathetic action.[18]

One can deny that God has knowledge of the future and the choices of free agents. Therefore, through His providence, He works through our brokenness to bring beautiful outcomes. Those beautiful outcomes include the development of our souls and becoming more conformed to the image of Christ. Therefore, even evils that God allows are meant to develop the soul. God deciding to act and bring about moral improvement providentially is the greater good that comes along with the allowance of free will.

---

17   Richard Swinburne, *Providence and the Problem of Evil* (New York: Oxford University Press, 1998), 161-162, Kindle Edition.

18   Ibid., 228.

Joni Eareckson Tada presents a similar case for soul-making. She argues her disability is used by God to not only make her a better person but make the people around her better as well. For example, even of her salvation, she writes,

> After forty years of quadriplegia, with my chronic pain and now shortness of breath, I can say, God will permit that broken heart. God will permit that broken home. God will permit that broken neck. Suffering then is like a sheep dog snapping at my heels, driving me down the road to Calvary, where otherwise I might not naturally be inclined to go.[19]

She has grown as a consequence of the trials she has gone through. She tells the story of her friend Steve who helped her when she was having a hard time accepting her physical situation. He said, and she expanded on, "'God permits what he hates in order to accomplish what he loves.' Heaven and hell can end up participating in the exact same event but for different reasons. Ephesians 1:11 puts it plainly: God 'according to [his] purpose ... works all things according to the counsel of his will.'"[20] There are times when events that seem to be evil, and perhaps are actually evil, are simultaneously good. As paradoxical as it seems, even if God allows evil, He will use evil for His glory and the development of the individual soul.

She argues that disability may be one of the most potent images of the reality of Jesus Christ in the church. In a claim that some will find controversial, she writes, "People with disabilities, unlike others, are driven to the cross by the overwhelming conviction that they have no other place to go."[21] While some may critique Eareckson Tada's statement as overly negative or hopeless, there is a great deal of truth in it. If someone struggles to accept disability, there is likely no escape from that condition. Most of the time, disability is not something that just disappears. Therefore, if there is no hope of changing an undesirable situation here, is it necessarily surprising that people with disabilities might be drawn towards God as a way to find the peace, hope, and joy that God has promised those who follow Him? Again, the presence of disability helps drive souls to God.

Notice the benefits of soul-making extend beyond just individuals with disabilities. Eareckson Tada argues that the church grows through faithful testimonies despite difficulties, and she even argues that the most mundane parts of her life can help others. She writes,

> When I hear my girlfriend in the kitchen running water for coffee, and I know she will come into the bedroom to give me a bed bath, get me dressed, and sit me up in my wheelchair, I'm thinking, "Oh, God, I'm so tired! I don't

---

19　Joni Eareckson Tada, "Redeeming Suffering," in *Why, O God?: Suffering and Disability in the Bible and the Church*, eds. Larry J. Waters and Roy B. Zuck (Wheaton: Crossway, 2001), Kindle Edition.

20　Ibid.

21　Ibid.

think I can face one more day of quadriplegia. I'm already thinking about how wonderful it will feel when my head is back on this pillow tonight. But, Lord, I need to give a smile to this girl who is ready to get me up. So, Lord Jesus, please give me your smile. I cannot 'do' quadriplegia, but I can do all things through you who strengthens me."[22]

Ironically, she can help the one who is helping her. Not only is Eareckson Tada blessed by the fact that she has someone to help her get ready for the day, but she can also encourage her assistant as well. The effect can permeate an entire church or community. Without Eareckson Tada, the body of Christ would certainly be different and not for the better. Her situation has strengthened the faith of many others.

Eareckson Tada's story is not an instance of the "disabled as inspiration" stereotype championed by the MDA Telethon and other organizations. It is not helpful to ascribe false virtue to someone simply because they happen to have a disability. It is not inspiring for an adult with a disability to go to a store; it is human. Hardwick calls this phenomenon "inspiration porn" and explains, "While [inspiration porn] seems like a way to honor people with disabilities, it can be quite dehumanizing, making them the saintly figures who are incapable of wrong. They become saints and symbols in the eyes of others, making them less than human and eventually less valuable to our communities of faith."[23] Eareckson Tada is not suggesting that living with a disability is inspirational either, even though she speaks of her disability being able to strengthen the faith of others. Instead, she recognizes that every person has a role to play in the body of Christ. We are all called to support one another. Eareckson Tada strengthens the faith of other people through her example as a mature Christian.

Any time a soul-making theodicy is considered, God is acting for His glory first and foremost. However, God is also working for the betterment of each individual person, even though he or she might not recognize it at the time. Only by going through terrifying experiences can one learn courage. Only by persevering through pain can one develop endurance. Only by smiling when all instincts seem to force tears can one develop inner strength to bless others even when times get dark. Experientially, all of these cause-and-effect relationships seem to prove true in individual lives. Because each of the outcomes is good, it also seems possible that God would allow free will and its subsequent evil consequences if, through those situations, He could draw people closer to Him at first in salvation and then in further sanctification.

---

22 Joni Eareckson Tada, "Wheelchairs in Heaven?" in *Why, O God?: Suffering and Disability in the Bible and the Church*, eds. Larry J. Waters and Roy B. Zuck (Wheaton: Crossway, 2001), Kindle Edition.

23 Lamar Hardwick, *Disability and the Church* (Downers Grove, IL: InterVarsity Press, 2021), 111, Kindle Edition.

C. Reformed Theodicies

As Reformed Christians will not affirm the concept of libertarian free will and will contend for compatibilist free will, they will require an argument that allows for God not to be the author of sin but to have a higher purpose for the existence of sin. God allows sin in the world for the existence of a greater good.

Joe Rigney points out the stark reality that "All things — good, bad, ugly, and horrific — are ordained, guided, and governed by the Creator and Sustainer of the universe."[24] He continues to lay out the analogy of an author and a story. He explains, "Every aspect of the story — from plot to characters to background details — is under the sovereign control of the Author. And the actions of the characters are necessary for the resolution of the plot."[25] Therefore, the Reformed perspective rejects the second premise that if God is entirely good, He will prevent all evil. For Rigney, "If the world is a story, then evil is really an example of narratival tension. Thus, we can see more clearly God's reasoning in permitting and ordaining that evil exist. God ordains evil for the same reason that Lewis creates the White Witch: so that Aslan will have someone to conquer."[26] Evil as tension is consistent with Owen Anderson's reminder of God's purpose in creation, based on the Westminster Confession, "God's purpose in creation was not to give humans a beatific vision or cultivate a relationship but was to manifest his glory."[27]

Understanding God's ultimate purpose in creation is important because, as Anderson points out, "The end of God's appointing this day is for the manifestation of the glory of His mercy, in the eternal salvation of the elect; and of His justice, in the damnation of the reprobate, who are wicked and disobedient."[28] However, the elect are not always going to have a straight road to their perfect destination. As the Westminster Confession says:

> The most wise, righteous, and gracious God doth oftentimes leave for a season His own children to manifold temptations, and the corruption of their own hearts, to chastise them for their former sins, or to discover unto them the hidden strength of corruption, and deceitfulness of their hearts, that they may be humbled; and, to raise them to a more close and constant dependence

---

24   Joe Rigney, "Confronting the Problem(s) of Evil," *Desiring God*, December 15, 2012, accessed December 28, 2020, https://www.desiringgod.org/articles/confronting-the-problems-of-evil.

25   Ibid.

26   Ibid.

27   Owen Anderson, "Free Will and Doxological Christianity," *DrOwenAnderson.com*, October 31, 2020, accessed December 28, 2020, https://drowenanderson.com/free-will-and-doxological-christianity/.

28   Ibid.

for their support upon Himself, and to make them more watchful against all future occasions of sin, and for sundry other just and holy ends.[29]

Being among the elect does not mean the avoidance of all trouble. On the contrary, God often uses all kinds of evil to help these people become closer to Him.

Consider the words of the Confession related to justification:

They who are once effectually called and regenerated, having a new heart and a new spirit created in them, are further sanctified, really and personally, through the virtue of Christ's death and resurrection, by His Word and Spirit dwelling in them: the dominion of the whole body of sin is destroyed, and the several lusts thereof are more and more weakened and mortified; and they more and more quickened and strengthened in all saving graces, to the practice of true holiness, without which no man shall see the Lord.[30]

The destruction of sin within us might not feel comforting. However, the sin being worked out of us only displays God's mercy and consequently His glory even more, which is the purpose of creation.

Returning to considering God as Divine Author then, natural and moral evil are used by God to develop the human soul, among other things. The consistent perseverance of the elect towards greater conformance to the person of Jesus Christ is only possible because there is evil to overcome. There would be nothing to persevere through without the existence of evil in the first place. What Rigney calls "narratival tension" points to the story God has written, and it is a story that humans are privileged to play a part in. God uses evil to glorify Himself, and part of that glorification is bringing humanity to a greater knowledge of His wonderful mercy, as well as His perfect justice.

Surrendra Gangadean has presented another Reformed solution to the problem of evil, and it is an approach that will be familiar to rational presuppositional apologists. Gangadean begins by defining good as that which is according to the nature of a being. Good for humans as rational beings is using reason to see what is clearly revealed to all about God. Evil is the failure to see what is clearly revealed about God. Gangadean writes, "Evil is not just objectively there in the world; it is subjectively here in the one asking the question."[31] Drawing from the Biblical parable of the prodigal son, he suggests that the son was entirely blind to the good father's way. Evil is the "failure to understand basic things

---

29   "The Westminster Confession of Faith (1647)," *Ligonier Ministries*, accessed December 28, 2020, https://www.ligonier.org/learn/articles/westminster-confession-faith/.

30   Ibid.

31   Surrendra Gangadean, *Philosophical Foundation: A Critical Analysis of Basic Beliefs* (Lanham, MD: University Press of America, 2008), 111.

which are clear."[32] The son did not realize the goodness of the father's way and was therefore not seeing reality clearly. He was committing moral evil. However, he ultimately came to his senses in the pigsty and began to see things clearly. He repented, realized his father's love at that point, and was able to experience his father's mercy by making the return trip to his father's house. Only when his perspective was rectified was he able to see that the way of his father was the right way, and he needed to reject his evil path. The natural evil he experienced through his uncomfortable flight from his father served to bring him to repentance for his moral evil.

The story of the prodigal son brings Gangadean to his conclusion. Just as the son was blind to the goodness of his father's way until his eyes were opened, those who say they cannot understand how there is evil in the world while also acknowledging the existence of God are similarly blind. He summarizes his contentions in four sentences:

1. Because of all the evil in the world I cannot see how it can be said that God is all good and all powerful.

2. Because of all the unbelief in the world I cannot see how it can be said that God is all good and all powerful.

3. Because of all the unbelief in me I cannot see how it can be said that God is all good and all powerful.

4. Because I have neglected and avoided the use of reason I cannot see what is clear about God.[33]

God has a purpose that He is orchestrating, and the problem of evil is not a problem for the rational presuppositionalist. The problem of evil is only a perceived problem because humans do not have clear vision. Because of our depraved limitations, we just do not understand how God is writing His grand story. Just because skeptics like Hume or Mackie can raise questions about God and His goodness does nothing to disprove God's goodness; their questions come from a place of ignorance driven by unbelief.

D. Conclusion

The problem of evil has been answered in three main ways: the free will defense, the soul-making theodicies, and the Reformed approaches. The first relies on the goodness of free will. Free will must be a great enough good for God to justify giving it as a gift to humanity despite all the evil caused by humans

---

32   Surrendra Gangadean, *Philosophical Foundation: A Critical Analysis of Basic Beliefs* (Lanham, MD: University Press of America, 2008), 111.

33   Ibid., 114.

who abuse that good gift. Soul-making theodicies depend on God using evil for a higher purpose. Whether God uses the evil that follows free choices and weaves the future into a beautiful pattern or whether God allows evil to create a tapestry that unrolls as a testament to His glory, a soul-making theodicy contends there is some purpose for evil that justifies its existence. Typically, this purpose results in the development of virtues that bring people closer to the image of Jesus Christ, like courage, forgiveness, love, peace, and self-control. Finally, Reformed approaches return to the contention that God orchestrates whatever happens in our world for His glory. While all three of these perspectives would affirm the ultimate purpose of any activity is the glory of God, Reformed answers more heavily emphasize the story of the world and evil as a narrative device, bringing glory to God.

From a free will perspective, disability is a consequence of our fallen world. Evil exists because humanity makes evil choices. Therefore, genetic mutations or car accidents are the consequences of evil. They exist in the world because humanity has done an extraordinary job at ruining the perfect world that was given in the first place. Human free will is responsible for moral evil and natural evil, causing the first evil that corrupted everything else. However, a world with free will, where people can make so many great and noble choices in the face of these difficulties, is a good enough world to offset the existence of these evils in the first place. A free world with great evil is better than a robotic world without love. God is glorified in His beautiful relationships with His children.

From a soul-making perspective, disability exists for the growth of the individual and, ultimately, the glory of God. Because of difficult situations, each individual has the opportunity to grow through them and become more conformed to the image of Jesus Christ. As a personal note, I believe that I have grown in many ways because of my disability, and I have often wondered if my personality would have developed in the same way if I had not been through the challenges I have experienced. It is quite possible that God, if we assume the soul-making theodicy, has given me this life in this time in this place with this disability for His glory. He may have put my disability in place and put me here for a purpose that is not be immediately evident to me, especially when I am dealing with difficult times. A soul-making theodicy provides another potential answer to the problem of evil.

A Reformed perspective focuses on the grand story of God's world. Everything that happens is part of God's narrative, no matter how it may appear to those of us who are living through it. Disability exists for the glory of God, which may not make sense and, frankly, does not need to. Asking questions of God from our human position that lacks clarity does not mean that those questions are reasonable. Whether we consider disability good, bad, or indifferent from our earthly perspective, the fact of the matter is that God has ordained disability for a particular role in His story for His glory. Therefore, when evaluating disability and the problem of evil from a Reformed perspective, it is no more of a problem than any other event in the history of the world.

The problem of evil has been a challenge for humanity since arguably the beginning of human existence. Even though there are differing opinions on how to answer the problem of evil among Christians, Daniel R. Thomson highlights a shared theme that runs through each of the methods mentioned above. He explains, "Believers, however, do know the Who, which makes it possible to endure temporary hardships as one maintains an eternal hope and biblical perspective toward the realities of life."[34] Each method comes equipped with a hopeful conclusion that there is a good God who made the universe the way it is. Therefore, when considering why things happen that do not seem to be consistent with the character of a good, all-knowing, all-powerful God, it is important to remember the many options that have developed to provide an answer and a reason for the existence of evil in the world.

---

34   Daniel R. Thomson, "A Biblical Disability-Ministry Perspective," in *Why, O God?: Suffering and Disability in the Bible and the Church*, eds. Larry J. Waters and Roy B. Zuck (Wheaton: Crossway, 2001), Kindle Edition.

Chapter 4

Biblical Perspectives on Disability

With definitions established for what disability and the problem of evil are, the next logical step for this book is to explore the Biblical testimony about these issues. Ros Bayes unequivocally states, "The Bible is full of people whose disabilities were no barrier to them playing a vital part in the history of God's people."[1] To develop a Christian response and understanding of the relationship between disability and the problem of evil, it certainly makes sense to consider God's revelation as shown in the Bible. Suffering and evil have been present in the universe for a very long time, and as such, there is no shortage of Biblical discussion about them. It is important to keep in mind that even if a particular author does not refer to disability specifically, considerations of suffering or evil, in general, can be potentially relevant to a discussion of disability on a case-by-case basis. While many disability rights activists might consider this an equivocation between disability and evil, that is not true. Rather, many disabilities do bring suffering along with them. That is simply reality, so it is worth viewing any passage relating to suffering to see if there is applicability for the discussion of disability.

Similarly, many people view disability as a type of natural evil. Again, many disability rights activists will cringe at the label of evil being applied in this context. Recall that natural evil is not the same as moral evil, though. It is not a moral judgment about the person who has a disability. Rather, natural evil speaks about difficult situations that arise in people's lives that are a consequence of nature. For example, for those who have genetic disabilities, natural evil is at play. It is a difficult situation that arises from being in the world in the same sense that a hurricane is a catastrophe that simply occurs. Therefore, passages that speak to natural evil and why God allows things to go wrong but are within the expansive power of God to control can potentially apply to disability as well.

Five different passages are going to be considered in this chapter. There are more cases of disability in the Bible, and this chapter does not intend to be comprehensive. However, these five examples have been chosen to illustrate different kinds of disability, different responses to disability, and different views of disability. First, the book of Job is the quintessential Biblical exploration of

---

1   Ros Bayes, "A Biblical View of Disability," *BeThinking*, 2015, accessed December 28, 2020, https://www.bethinking.org/human-life/a-biblical-view-of-disability.

suffering. It shows how God and man relate to suffering. Second, several Psalms will provide a human perspective on experiencing suffering. Third, the Gospels portray Jesus as the suffering Savior; God does not only talk about suffering and evil, but God experienced them as a man. Next, the letters of Paul show a first-hand perspective of a man most likely living with a disability. Finally, the ending of Revelation pictures a future where there will be no more pain, which naturally has implications for speaking about the current existence of suffering and evil. These five passages will provide a representative sample of the Biblical testimony on disability which can inform modern-day discussions of disability and how the problem of evil is answered from a Christian worldview.

A. Job

Job was a man who had many earthly blessings, and Satan believed he was only faithful to God because of all of those blessings. God then gave Satan permission to do whatever he wanted to Job short of touching him, so he proceeded to kill many of Job's servants, his livestock, and even his children.[2] Job was distraught, but "In all this Job did not sin or charge God with wrong."[3] It is important to recognize that sorrow is not sinful. Job was able to grieve for those people who died. Sinless grief was not the reaction that Satan was looking for, however, because when God and Satan spoke again, Satan wanted to change the conditions that God laid out. "Skin for skin! All that a man has he will give for his life. But stretch out your hand and touch his bone and his flesh, and he will curse you to your face."[4] This time, God only demands that Satan cannot kill Job. "So Satan went out from the presence of the LORD and struck Job with loathsome sores from the sole of his foot to the crown of his head."[5] Of all of the difficulties Job experiences, Anderson claims that this moment, sitting in great pain on ashes, is "the bottom" for Job.[6] He experiences disability as he is afflicted by a condition that is making his life much more difficult. Using the terminology of the definition of disability used in this book, Job's condition was a disability because the pain he was experiencing was an impairment that surely interfered with completing major life activities.

It is true that at the end of the book of Job, these sores disappear, so his circumstance might not qualify perfectly for the definition of disability that is being used in this book because it is not long-term.[7] Job had no idea that he

---

2   Job 1:14-19, ESV.

3   Job 1:22, ESV.

4   Job 2:4-5, ESV.

5   Job 2:7, ESV.

6   Owen Anderson, *Job: A Philosophical Commentary* (Phoenix: Logos Papers Press, 2021), 24.

7   Job 42:10, ESV.

would ever be made well again, though, so, in that sense, Job would have lived as one with a disability. At least in his mind, he needed to come to terms with the fact that he might have to live the rest of his life with painful sores on his skin.

Whether or not Job truly meets the definition of a disability in the situation is somewhat beside the point, however. What is more important is to examine the portrayal of suffering. Job and his three friends raised serious questions about why God might allow suffering. His first friend, Eliphaz, suggests that all of Job's suffering is a consequence of the sin in his life. Eliphaz says, "Behold, blessed is the one whom God reproves; therefore despise not the discipline of the Almighty. For he wounds, but he binds up; he shatters, but his hands heal. He will deliver you from six troubles; in seven no evil shall touch you."[8] Assuming that Job's condition is a consequence of personal sin is problematic. Is it perhaps the case that God is simply bringing a form of judgment on an individual's life? It certainly is possible. God has judged people before, and He is going to judge all of humanity again. Therefore, it is not unbelievable to present a situation where disability is a type of divine punishment.

Job, however, has a very important request for Eliphaz. "Teach me, and I will be silent; make me understand how I have gone astray."[9] Job's wondering is very similar to the way many people with disabilities wonder about their own lives. Is it possible that disability is some extraordinary punishment based on personal sin? Like Saul on the road to Damascus, God has used disability as judgment. However, there was an apparent reason for Saul who hears, "I am Jesus, whom you are persecuting."[10] Saul had been directly persecuting the young church, and Job's question would be easy to answer in Saul's context. For many people with disabilities, while indeed still sinners like everyone else in the world, there would not be this kind of egregious behavior to report.

Consequently, Job's conversation with Eliphaz shows that it is far too simple to draw a correlation between the presence of suffering and the presence of egregious individual sin. Actions have consequences, and sinful actions do have bad consequences, if not on earth, then at least eternally. However, there are also times, like in Job, where the evidence does not appear nearly as clear. It is reasonable to conclude that while judgment can come in the form of a disability resulting from sin, it is not a necessary condition. Therefore, it is not enough to say that extraordinary suffering is always, or even often, a consequence of an extraordinary amount of individual personal sin.

Job's second friend Bildad could not accept this question from Job. "How long will you say these things, and the words of your mouth be a great wind? Does God pervert justice? Or does the Almighty pervert the right?"[11] No matter what

---

8 Job 5:17-19, ESV.

9 Job 6:24, ESV.

10 Acts 9:5, ESV.

11 Job 8:2-3, ESV.

Job said, Bildad understood his charge to be a direct assault on the justice of God. The Bible speaks of a God who is perfectly just, so for Bildad, it is not appropriate to question why God is doing what He is doing. After all, by default, God must have a reason for doing it, and by definition, that reason will be just. Anderson summarizes Bildad's argument as a simple formula, "If you are innocent, you will not suffer. You are suffering, so you are not innocent."[12]

However, it is important to recognize that Job did not deny there might be a possible reason for God to allow suffering in his life, but he wanted to be shown what that reason was. It is a subtle difference, but it is one that Job tries to draw out in his response. "Though I am in the right, my own mouth would condemn me; though I am blameless, he would prove me perverse."[13] Job fully understood that he was not perfect. However, he similarly believed that in this situation, he was entirely right. Most people ought to be able to identify with this conflict. It is one thing to understand the characteristics and attributes of God. It is another thing to feel justified in a specific situation. It is a disconnect between the emotional and the intellectual, but it brings Job back to his fundamental question. "I will say to God, Do not condemn me; let me know why you contend against me."[14]

Understanding why God allows evil is of chief importance for a soul-making theodicy. These theodicies trust in God's justice as well as the overarching goodness of the story God is writing for His glory in the history of the world. Consequently, there needs to be a reason why Job needs to suffer. Job does not deny the possibility of soul-making; there could be something about this difficulty in his life that will bring glory to God through Job's spiritual growth. He faces a more emotional problem here, something that individuals with disabilities might feel from time to time. Even as Christians, we want answers for why things are the way they are. If God told us outright that he was going to use our circumstances for some specific amazing purpose, we could take comfort in the fact that a greater good was going to emerge. However, even while affirming this answer to the problem of evil, it can be challenging to rest in these general promises as the answer to a specific situation. It is not a logical problem, but it is truly an emotional problem.

Zophar is the third of Job's friends to come to counsel him, but the message has not really changed. "Can you find out the deep things of God? Can you find out the limit of the Almighty? It is higher than heaven — what can you do? Deeper than Sheol — what can you know?"[15] Again, Zophar suggests it is entirely possible that God has a reason for his suffering, and Job, as a limited man, might not be able to understand the reason. Zophar has a prescription for Job to move beyond this problem. "If you prepare your heart, you will stretch out your hands toward

---

12   Owen Anderson, *Job: A Philosophical Commentary* (Phoenix: Logos Papers Press, 2021), 47.

13   Job 9:20, ESV.

14   Job 10:2, ESV.

15   Job 11:7-8, ESV.

him. If iniquity is in your hand, put it far away, and let not injustice dwell in your tents. Surely then you will lift up your face without blemish; you will be secure and will not fear."[16] He understood that Job would deny any wrongdoing, so he creates a conditional statement about the possibility of sin and encourages Job to put it far away if it exists. The insinuation is that it does exist, but Zophar knows enough not to accuse Job directly at this point. Job simply does not have time for any more advice.

> But I have understanding as well as you; I am not inferior to you. Who does not know such things as these? I am a laughingstock to my friends; I, who called to God and he answered me, a just and blameless man, am a laughingstock . . . The tents of robbers are at peace, and those who provoke God are secure, who bring their god in their hand.[17]

He knew that it felt strange that he was following God and received sorrow while those who were visibly committing offenses against God lived at peace. He could not understand what was going on, and even though he went through further questioning with these three friends, they were unable to find agreement.

When I reflect on Job's disability, I cannot help but think about individuals who are injured in automobile accidents with drunk drivers. The one who did the crime is unchanged by the experience, except hopefully booked with criminal charges, but another person has to live with massive life changes. It simply does not seem right that someone who did nothing wrong suffers the consequences of the actions of someone who chose to do wrong. This situation seems especially challenging for those who would embrace a free will defense, although it applies to a soul-making theodicy as well. One person utilized his or her free will, a great good, to do something that was evil. It seems like there is an imbalance here; the good of free will does not seem to outweigh the evil of its abuse. Job's frustration, again, is emotional rather than logical, but it is a very real and relatable frustration.

Elihu then comes to counsel Job. He brings a different perspective that Larry J. Waters outlines. Waters suggests that Elihu taught Job

> his suffering was not because of past sin, but was (1) to keep Job from continuing to accept a sinful premise for suffering, (2) to draw him closer to God, (3) to teach him a true wisdom that reveals God as sovereignly in control of the affairs of life, and (4) to show that God does reward the righteous, but only on the basis of his love and grace.[18]

Elihu reframes the entire issue. Job continually contended that he knew that he had no extenuating circumstances that would make him especially deserving of punishment from God. He knew he was not perfect, but he wanted to know

---

16   Job 11:13-15, ESV.

17   Job 12:3-4, 6, ESV.

18   Larry J. Waters, "Suffering in the Book of Job," in *Why, O God?: Suffering and Disability in the Bible and the Church*, eds. Larry J. Waters and Roy B. Zuck (Wheaton: Crossway, 2001), Kindle Edition.

why God thought it just to bring such severe judgment on him. He repeatedly argued that his disability was not a prescription to fix the moral evil in his life. Elihu understood that and presented a new perspective. Maybe there are other reasons for suffering besides the punishment of sin. Perhaps there are redeeming qualities to suffering that God could use for a greater good. Anderson explains that Elihu "is not some kind of supernatural being, and he pointed to the need for God to make things right."[19] Any soul-making theodicy or Reformed approach is going to make a very similar argument. Perhaps there is a reason why God allows disability to affect people who are sincerely trying to follow Him. It does not make it pleasant or comfortable, but it is at least logically possible that a greater good could emerge from the presence of the disability Job experienced.

Elihu understands the suffering that Job is going through. Of course, he does not have firsthand knowledge of Job's specific circumstances, but he understands that all people experience suffering while on earth. It is simply a fact of nature. "Man is also rebuked with pain on his bed and with continual strife in his bones, so that his life loathes bread, and his appetite the choicest food. His flesh is so wasted away that it cannot be seen, and his bones that were not seen stick out. His soul draws near the pit, and his life to those who bring death."[20] In difficult times, it is easy for anyone to "draw near the pit." They begin to abandon their faith in God because of the terrible pain. They allow their circumstances to influence their commitment to God, and they start to stray from where they need to be. For some, disability can appear to be a sign of God abandoning them. Christians understand that God will never leave them, but as many of the Psalms can attest, it does not always feel like God is right there. In those moments of spiritual darkness, it is tempting to give in to despair. It is in times like these that conversations about the problem of evil start to take shape.

Elihu points out that through this suffering, there is the opportunity for growth and spiritual development. He provides support for one of the chief claims behind a soul-making theodicy.

> If there be for him an angel, a mediator, one of the thousand, to declare to man what is right for him, and he is merciful to him, and says, 'Deliver him from going down into the pit; I have found a ransom; let his flesh become fresh with youth; let him return to the days of his youthful vigor'; then man prays to God, and he accepts him; he sees his face with a shout of joy, and he restores to man his righteousness.[21]

Elihu himself is playing the role of mediator in the life of Job. He is stepping between Job and God. Granted, he is not a perfect mediator, but he is trying to provide clarity. He is trying to help Job put things in the proper perspective and avoid sin.

---

19   Owen Anderson, *Job: A Philosophical Commentary* (Phoenix: Logos Papers Press, 2021), 134.

20   Job 33:19-22, ESV.

21   Job 33:23-26, ESV.

When the man in Elihu's illustration recognizes that he is allowing his suffering to draw him too close to the pit, he prays to God and realizes that his true joy is in the righteousness that God restores to him. There is no mention of physical healing in this passage; his disability is still present. The man is delighted because he has been reconciled to God, and God has given him his righteousness.

> He sings before men and says: "I sinned and perverted what was right, and it was not repaid to me. He has redeemed my soul from going down into the pit, and my life shall look upon the light. Behold, God does all these things, twice, three times, with a man, to bring back his soul from the pit, that he may be lighted with the light of life."[22]

Elihu requires spiritual reconciliation for true healing. This passage is almost a perfect illustration of a soul-making theodicy. First of all, the man has avoided the sin of cursing God. The man has nearly fallen into the pit, but ultimately, he gains a proper perspective with the assistance of those around him. Second, as shown by the joy at the end of this passage, there is no doubt that the man had a more fulfilling relationship with God after going through trials. It was not that it was easy by any means, and this passage does not try to minimize what suffering he endured, but his painful circumstances also blessed him.

Elihu's proverbial man had a terrible illness that was causing him pain, but he was able to rejoice because God was in control and was able to save him from descending into the pit. In other words, he began to understand that there were things that were much more important than temporal health and comfort. Specifically, it was more important that God was in control and ultimately glorified. Finally, it also shows that God was still providing for this man even in these difficult times. There is no indication that his suffering went away. His health was still failing, but God gave him joy. He was rewarded for making the right decision. It might not have been the reward that the world was looking for, but it was a reward that came from viewing the situation appropriately.

Waters interprets this dialogue with Elihu by saying, "Since God goes to such lengths to develop this relationship, suffering becomes the supreme opportunity for humans to represent this relationship with God to the world."[23] Waters' view parallels the beginning of the book of Job. There was a reason for the suffering of Job, and God allowed Satan to do his worst. God had Satan consider Job because of the relationship between God and Job. Job was "a blameless and upright man, who fears God and turns away from evil."[24] The reader of Job knows the background challenge that Job himself did not know at the time. Job did not suffer because of personal evil; the reason for Job's suffering was to bring about the ultimate glory of God. Elihu provides a balance to Job's other friends' condemnation and comes

---

22 Job 33:27-30, ESV.

23 Larry J. Waters, "Suffering in the Book of Job," in *Why, O God?: Suffering and Disability in the Bible and the Church*, eds. Larry J. Waters and Roy B. Zuck (Wheaton: Crossway, 2001), Kindle Edition.

24 Job 1:8, ESV.

closer to the actual truth. Job's disability was not punishment for previous sins; there was another reason for God allowing this difficulty in his life.

At the end of the book of Job, God responds to Job out of the whirlwind. Interestingly, God never provides a complete answer to Job as to why everything had happened in the way that it did. The one thing that Job wanted from the beginning was the one thing that he did not receive. Rather, God poses a series of challenges, the first of which Job cannot provide a satisfactory answer to. "Where were you when I laid the foundation of the earth? Tell me, if you have understanding. Who determined its measurements — surely you know! Or who stretched the line upon it?"[25] Job would have been only able to answer these questions in one way. God did all of those things. It certainly was not Job himself, and God was the one who had orchestrated the universe from the beginning. After God provides several examples of things that He had done throughout the universe, he asks Job to comment, and Job decides that his best option is not to speak. "Behold, I am of small account; what shall I answer you? I lay my hand on my mouth. I have spoken once, and I will not answer; twice, but I will proceed no further."[26]

After God continues providing more examples, Job comes to a significant conclusion about his relationship to God.

> I know that you can do all things, and that no purpose of yours can be thwarted. 'Who is this that hides counsel without knowledge?' Therefore I have uttered what I did not understand, things too wonderful for me, which I did not know. 'Hear, and I will speak; I will question you, and you make it known to me.' I had heard of you by the hearing of the ear, but now my eye sees you; therefore I despise myself, and repent in dust and ashes.[27]

Job has spent most of his time questioning why God has allowed certain things to happen to him. He did not sin by questioning, but he did doubt the justice of God. In fact, it is worth noting, as pointed out by Bayes, "It was not, in fact, God who had taken away but it was God who restored to him more than he had lost."[28] Everything was restored to Job in the end; Satan had taken it away, but God purposed to give everything back to Job and then some.

Job recognizes the purposes of God cannot be undone. They cannot be thwarted by evil, and Job's revelation can be attributed to the testimony of Elihu as well as the voice of God Himself. Job understands that there are things about God that he is not capable of understanding. Logically, it makes sense that a human

---

25   Job 38:4-5, ESV.

26   Job 40:4-5, ESV.

27   Job 42:2-6, ESV.

28   Ros Bayes, "A Biblical View of Disability," *BeThinking*, 2015, accessed December 28, 2020, https://www.bethinking.org/human-life/a-biblical-view-of-disability.

would be incapable of completely understanding God. God is, by definition, an infinite being with knowledge of everything. Humans are finite beings who have limited intellectual abilities and cannot understand everything in the same way God can. Therefore, it is not surprising that Job has to admit that there are things that are too wonderful for him to understand. It does not mean that God is not just, and it does not make God evil. It is a recognition of reality.

It is possible that God may have a purpose for allowing disability. It might be a good purpose. What that does not guarantee is that people will immediately know that purpose. In fact, the purpose might not ever be known. God might not disclose that purpose today in the way that He did not disclose His purpose to Job immediately. However, like Job, people with disabilities are finite people, and it would not be surprising in the least to see God have a purpose that people are just not able to understand.

The story of Job comfortably fits with all three ways to consider the problem of evil. The fact that God invites Satan to tempt Job suggests that Job can reject God. If Job has free will, humanity, in general, has free will, which returns the question to why God created humanity in that way and therefore allowed the human race to fall into evil. From a soul-making perspective, Job grows through encountering God and learns something of the nature of God by the end of his story. A soul-making theodicy is probably the most directly applicable theological method to Job's situation. Finally, a Reformed perspective sees the narrative and understands that Job withstanding Satan's temptations was part of a story that brought glory to God.

The book of Job arguably provides the most direct commentary on suffering and the human condition in the Bible. By viewing a man who was suffering horribly, the problem of evil is the focus of the text. Why does God allow severe suffering to fall on one who, by any human standard, has done nothing egregiously evil? Ultimately, God answers that He is God. It is not a direct explanation, but it brings up an important consideration for exploring the problem of evil in relation to disability. Gregory A. Hatteberg compares his wife's experience with multiple sclerosis to Job and recognizes, "Sometimes we sound like Job asking the questions God never intends to answer this side of heaven. But we are thankful that while we may not have the answers, he does give us a purpose. His glory."[29] Answers are not always given, even when we feel like we are entitled to them. Rather, we a given a mission that we can pursue, no matter what our earthly circumstances.

There are times when God makes explanations rather obvious. Sodom and Gomorrah are clear examples.[30] There was great evil, and God brought judgment and suffering by destroying the cities. In the case of Job, however, blatant, moral

---

29 Gregory A. Hatteberg, "The Rolling Throne," in *Why, O God?: Suffering and Disability in the Bible and the Church*, eds. Larry J. Waters and Roy B. Zuck (Wheaton: Crossway, 2001), Kindle Edition.

30 Genesis 19:1-29, ESV.

evil does not seem to be there. The reader knows God is using Job's suffering at the hands of Satan for His glory from the beginning of the book, but Job does not know it at the time. Job asks his friends and God many questions, like most of us would in a similar situation. God's ultimate answer is the reassurance of His control and His character. Job's story directly confronts Hume's claim that God is malevolent; Job learns that God is not malevolent and is blessed for his faith.

B. Psalms

A majority of the Psalms were written by David, a man acquainted with suffering. There is no record of David having any disability. Instead, his suffering was often related to his sin and came from various moral and natural causes. He did have an experience with disability after the death of King Saul. David wanted to show kindness to a descendant of Saul's house, and the only member left was Mephibosheth. He happened to be unable to walk, and David treated him as one of his own sons.[31] It is hard to identify when this event took place in relation to the many Psalms David wrote, but, at the very least, he did have some direct experience with disability.

David himself suffered through his circumstances. He was a man with many enemies. Whether it was King Saul early in his life or his son Absalom later in life, he was often pursued and lived in great danger. His suffering is not specifically related to disability, but it shows how David endured. Different kinds of troubles are hard to compare to one another, so it is incorrect to say that his pursuit by armies is the same as disability. That being said, suffering generally evokes certain emotions, so there is a connection from the Psalms to disability. They both can express the range of emotions felt while suffering. David's writing demonstrates his relationship with God and how he cries out to God in difficult times.

Psalm 22 provides an example of David's feelings of abandonment. "My God, my God, why have you forsaken me? Why are you so far from saving me, from the words of my groaning?"[32] Interestingly, these are the same words that Jesus Christ would later speak on the cross, but they portray a man who has nowhere left to turn. "O my God, I cry by day, but you do not answer, and by night, but I find no rest. Yet you are holy, enthroned on the praises of Israel."[33] David plainly states the problem of evil. He is experiencing evil in his life, and he feels that God has left him. He understands that God is holy, he understands that God is not evil, and he understands that God is listening to him. However, for some reason, God has chosen not to answer his specific prayer. If all of David's statements about God are true, why is there evil?

---

31 2 Samuel 9:11-13, ESV.

32 Psalms 22:1, ESV.

33 Psalms 22:2-3, ESV.

As an Israelite, he understood that God had delivered the people many times.[34] People with disabilities have also been miraculously healed innumerable times throughout history.[35] As will soon be shown in the Gospels, God is certainly more than capable of healing whatever disability a person might have. Just as He did in the history of Israel, God can move, and God can act powerfully. God continues to act powerfully today. However, God does not always act in the way that we want or expect Him to, and David soon became an object of ridicule for those around him. "All who see me mock me; they make mouths at me; they wag their heads; 'He trusts in the LORD; let him deliver him; let him rescue him, for he delights in him!'"[36] Everyone expected a God who was perfectly good to act in a certain way, and when He did not deliver in that manner, they started to mock those who had put their trust in Him.

Much like Job's friends, David's mockers do not understand how God can be good while simultaneously not answering his prayers. More is known of David's history than Job's, and there are chapters in David's story that clearly illustrate his sinfulness. Therefore, one could make the case that David might be experiencing a form of moral judgment that Job, a seemingly more righteous man, would not have brought upon himself. However, this supposition presents theological difficulties. Job and David were both sinners because they were human. Anyone receiving a blessing from God is as much of a sinner as anyone who feels forsaken by God. David's detractors do not argue that God is judging him for his sins, though. They mocked David because he put his faith in God, and God did not seem to be answering him.

Despite the scorners and suffering, David still felt that he had to call out to God. His desire is shown at the beginning of the Psalm and also throughout the rest of the passage. "But you, O LORD, do not be far off! O you my help, come quickly to my aid! Deliver my soul from the sword, my precious life from the power of the dog!"[37] Even though he felt like God had abandoned him and even though he had not heard a perceptible answer from God, he calls out to God. He does not demand anything of God, but he makes a request. He comes before God and asks for His assistance through the storm. Reaching out to someone we believe is in control when everything is spiraling uncontrollably is a general human impulse.

David promises to acknowledge God publicly and will not let the deliverance of God slip into oblivion. If God was going to deliver him from this circumstance, he would go public with his praise.

---

34   Psalms 22:4-5, ESV.

35   For more detail on miracle claims, see Craig S. Keener, *Miracles: The Credibility of the New Testament* (Grand Rapids: Baker Academic, 2011).

36   Psalms 22:7-8, ESV.

37   Psalms 22:19-20, ESV.

I will tell of your name to my brothers; in the midst of the congregation I will praise you: You who fear the LORD, praise him! All you offspring of Jacob, glorify him, and stand in awe of him, all you offspring of Israel! For he has not despised or abhorred the affliction of the afflicted, and he has not hidden his face from him, but has heard, when he cried to him.[38]

He promises to make sure that God receives all of the glory for the deliverance. The deliverance would not come because David was a great man. "All the ends of the earth shall remember and turn to the LORD, and all the families of the nations shall worship before you."[39]

The similarities between this Psalm and Job are quite striking. This Psalm is a lament written by David, and there is no direct response from God as is found in Job. However, David was a man who was trying to follow God just as Job was. He was not perfect, but he was trying to live a life that was in accordance with the will of God. David found himself in a situation where everything was going wrong, and even though he was looking for an explanation from God, no answer came. Job wanted to know why God allowed so many terrible things to happen to him, and until the end of the book, he did not receive an answer either. Even though God did respond at the end, it was probably not the type of answer Job desired. God never gave a specific reason but simply reaffirmed that He was God and was in control.

Individuals with disabilities might feel the same way at times. Moral and natural evil pile up around them. I have heard far too many stories from people with disabilities who feel abandoned, forgotten, lonely, neglected, and even broken. I will not tell specifics, but this is an extraordinarily real and common experience in the disability community. As the evil seems to become more powerful, hope seems to diminish, and feelings of abandonment grow. It is easy to ask God for a particular answer to prayer, but it is much harder to wait for the response or not receive the desired solution. It might feel like God has gone silent, and, like in the time of David, the world is eager to accuse God of failure. However, no matter how much it feels like God has disappeared, the situation is not nearly that bleak. God is still there, and God is still good even if human minds and hearts cannot always perceive His presence.

David's Psalms also provide a reminder that those who follow Christ can have confidence despite the circumstances they find themselves in. Even when enemies surrounded David, he was willing to call on God for salvation because he knew God would hear. "O LORD, how many are my foes! Many are rising against me; many are saying of my soul, there is no salvation for him in God. Selah. But you, O LORD, are a shield about me, my glory, and the lifter of my head. I cried aloud to the LORD, and he answered me from his holy hill. Selah."[40]

---

38   Psalms 22:22-24, ESV.

39   Psalms 22:27, ESV.

40   Psalms 3:1-4, ESV.

David knew the situation that he was in just as people with disabilities clearly understand the position that they find themselves in. As a warrior, he understood an unfavorable battlefield when he saw it. Frightening circumstances can lead to feelings of discouragement. Living life with a disability can be hard, and there are times when facing that reality is not as easy as it is at other times. However, even when he was afraid and mocked, David cried out to God because he knew God would answer. Psalm 3 is slightly different than Psalm 22 because there is an indication here that God did answer. Although David does not explain what kind of answer he received from God, he had confidence that was again upheld by whatever response he did receive. "Salvation belongs to the LORD; your blessing be on your people! Selah."[41] He knew that despite the circumstances he was in and even though his enemies were all around him, God was in control of the entire situation.

Admittedly, this Psalm does not provide a perfect parallel to disability for a few reasons. First of all, a disability is not necessarily an enemy. Although disabilities might make certain major life activities more difficult, many people would contend that it is not an enemy but rather a part of their identity. I may be who I am because of my disability. Yes, it is a challenge, but I don't know who I would be without it. Therefore, it is not something that is always my enemy. Using the word enemy seems to convey a sense of constant opposition that I don't know is always present, at least in my own life, even though I believe disability is a consequence of evil in the world. Life with a disability is full of plenty of joyous moments as well.

Secondly, deliverance from a disability looks different than David's deliverance from an enemy. David was praying for rescue from his enemies. The result that he was seeking was rather obvious, and evidence of God's providence was easy to measure. Most people with disabilities do not experience miraculous healing, so even if a person wants to be healed from his or her disability, this Psalm might not provide much comfort. While there is plenty of evidence of God performing miracles and bringing healing, it does not happen in every case, no matter how much faith and fervent prayer accompany the request. Much like the mockers in these two Psalms, critics say something must be wrong because God has healed people in the past but not now. Specific definitions of deliverance and salvation bring back the final dilemma of the problem of evil: why has God not acted if there is every indication that He could?

Psalms are complex because they are mirrors of human experience. Ronald B. Allen summed up the concept behind Psalms of lament by stating that they "express what one feels at the time of distress. One's feelings are in a blender. Everything is a whirl. One says all kinds of things, and among them are words

---

41   Psalms 3:8, ESV.

of confidence and expressions of distress."[42] Individuals with disabilities often experience similar emotional tension when wrestling with the meaning and purpose behind the existence of disability. Even though these Psalms were not written in the context of disability, many people with disabilities can relate to David's conflicting emotions of confidence and distress.

It is important to clarify that a life with a disability is far from a life of constant lament. Much like David's life, and much like everyone's, there are good and bad times. Those vicissitudes are part of being human no matter where you find yourself. However, disability is somewhat unique because it is easy to point to a specific, challenging circumstance. Disability is also a long-term challenge that often cannot be fixed. Many people with disabilities experience the problem of evil in the context of their identity-shaping disability. That is why it is so important to talk about the problem of evil in the context of disability. It is a different question than many other discussions on the problem of evil; it is often a question of who we are rather than why things happen to us.

Christians with disabilities have confidence in Jesus Christ. Faith is what makes them Christians. They have come to the cross and understand that Jesus Christ is their personal Lord and Savior. Just like individuals without disabilities, the promise is the same. At the same time, there are moments of distress when people become frustrated. Experientially, everyone becomes frustrated, but for people with disabilities, by definition, it can be difficult even to perform major life activities. It is not the same as the frustration of someone who cannot lift a three-hundred-pound barbell at the gym. Lifting that kind of weight is certainly not a normal, major life activity. Lifting a fork to eat dinner is a major life activity, and everyday frustrations can cause distress. Seeing everyone else can do something that you cannot do causes a deeper, personal frustration. Therefore, the integration of Christianity and disability is complex when viewed through the lens of the Psalms. Even though the Psalms might not seem to have much direct application to disability, it does provide insight into what it feels like to be going through trials and wondering when God will come in for the rescue.

C. The Gospels

Jesus Christ lived on earth for approximately thirty-three years. He was fully God and fully man. While there is no indication that He had any particular disability, He understood what it was like to experience physical pain and emotional stress. Roman crucifixion was one of the most brutal forms of execution in history, and before Jesus was crucified, He was beaten and humiliated. Almost all of His friends had abandoned Him, and even one of His most steadfast followers denied knowing Him. A member of His innermost circle betrayed Him.

---

42 Ronald B. Allen, "Suffering in the Psalms and Wisdom Books," in *Why, O God?: Suffering and Disability in the Bible and the Church*, eds. Larry J. Waters and Roy B. Zuck (Wheaton: Crossway, 2001), Kindle Edition.

When considering what Jesus endured to bring salvation to all who would freely accept it, it is humbling, to say the least. He was a perfectly innocent man who took the sins of the world upon Himself simply because of love.[43] The glory of God shone through that love, and His flawless character is demonstrated through the sacrifice He made for us.

Jesus provides a different example than Job and David. Job did not necessarily understand why he was going through what he was going through. He knew that he did not commit any particularly egregious sin that would bring about such a harsh round of judgment, but Job was still a sinner. As a man living in a world cursed by sin ever since the original fall in the Garden of Eden, Job was not perfect since Jesus Christ is the only one who was.[44] Similarly, David was a man whose errors are plainly recorded in the Bible. Therefore, being a sinner in a sinful world would bring about certain consequences for him as well. While there may be questions of degree and the appropriateness of the evil they encountered due to their relative levels of sin, being sinners who live in an imperfect world brings about consequences for either their own actions or the actions of others who have committed evil.

Jesus Christ, on the other hand, was perfect. There was no moral evil in Him. He did not bring evil onto Himself through bad decisions. Jesus did experience natural evil when He was in the midst of the storm on the Sea of Galilee.[45] He experienced evil in the world around Him, and He was betrayed by one who claimed to love Him in a display of moral evil.[46] It is not that Jesus was not surrounded by evil, but because He was morally perfect Himself, the penalty of sin would not need to apply to Him in the way that it applies to every other person in history. Everyone else has done wrong things and has deviated from the will of God. Jesus never sinned, and because there was no violation, He was entirely innocent of that burden. However, because He willingly took on the sins of the world and died to provide forgiveness for all sin, He had to suffer.

"Then Pilate took Jesus and flogged him. And the soldiers twisted together a crown of thorns and put it on his head and arrayed him in a purple robe."[47] Before the crucifixion, Jesus was tortured. Roman soldiers beat Him severely, and yet He persevered. He did not stray from the mission that God had ordained for Him. Jesus did not need to remain in this condition; as He said in the Garden of Gethsemane, angels were available at a moment's notice.[48] Consider the rest of His ministry. Jesus had healed many people. According to Mark Bailey, "Jesus worked four kinds of miracles: nine miracles in nature, seventeen healings, six

---

43   John 3:16, ESV.

44   Hebrews 4:15, ESV.

45   Mark 4:35-41, ESV.

46   Matthew 26:48-50, ESV.

47   John 19:1-2, ESV.

48   Matthew 26:53, ESV.

exorcisms, and three raisings from the dead."[49] There was no doubt that Jesus could relieve and avoid suffering. He had more than enough power to get off the cross. He demonstrated His power through miracles, but He made the conscious decision not to use His power and followed the will of God the Father. He remained voluntarily disabled because it was the will of God that He went through with this mission. Jacober states, "It is in the broken body of Jesus that inclusion is modeled. It is in Jesus that God incarnate is disabled … For all who have felt accursed, who have been labeled as less-than or unacceptable, what Jesus does on the cross is break the curse."[50] God became like each one of us willingly. Those who live in pain can rest assured that Jesus Christ experienced pain and understands suffering.

Jesus' mission was most likely even more difficult because using His power to leave the cross was what many of those around Jesus urged Him sarcastically to do. "The soldiers also mocked him, coming up and offering him sour wine and saying, 'If you are the King of the Jews, save yourself!'"[51] The soldiers were making fun of Him, but they would have known by the sign on His cross that He was accused of claiming He was the Messiah. They would not have believed He had that type of power, but His fame preceded Him with at least one of the other criminals who was being crucified with Him. "One of the criminals who were hanged railed at him, saying, 'Are you not the Christ? Save yourself and us!'"[52] The man was also mocking Jesus, but it shows Jesus' supposed power was known. People knew who He claimed to be.

Under this type of pressure, He was surely tempted to avoid this suffering, yet Jesus decided to continue following the will of His Father. There was purpose in the suffering of Jesus Christ. If everything Jesus did was in line with the will of the Father, and if He could fulfill His role perfectly, then it follows that suffering on the cross was also in line with the will of the Father. The prophet Isaiah points out why Jesus had to suffer, "Surely he has borne our griefs and carried our sorrows; yet we esteemed him stricken, smitten by God, and afflicted. But he was pierced for our transgressions; he was crushed for our iniquities; upon him was the chastisement that brought us peace, and with his wounds we are healed."[53] Jesus was bruised because of human sin. Jesus had to suffer because someone had to pay the penalty, and it was a penalty that no other human being was able to pay. All had fallen short, and Jesus was uniquely qualified to be the perfect sacrifice. As a result, God ordained a purpose behind even the suffering of His own obedient

---

49   Mark L. Bailey, "A Biblical Theology of Suffering in the Gospels," in *Why, O God?: Suffering and Disability in the Bible and the Church,* eds. Larry J. Waters and Roy B. Zuck (Wheaton: Crossway, 2001), Kindle Edition.

50   Amy E. Jacober, *Redefining Perfect: The Interplay Between Theology and Disability* (Eugene, OR: Cascade Books, 2017), chap. 2, Kindle Edition.

51   Luke 23:36-37, ESV.

52   Luke 23:39, ESV.

53   Isaiah 53:4-5, ESV.

Son. How much more could it be possible that God has a purpose behind every difficult circumstance in the lives of people with disabilities today?

Suggesting that there is a humanly unknown purpose behind all disabilities might seem to minimize the individual's experience. However, this is an emotional concern rather than a logical concern. God had a purpose for His own Son that involved suffering. Therefore, God is capable of allowing suffering for a purpose. That purpose was good. Therefore, God is capable of allowing suffering for a good purpose. If God could allow suffering for a good purpose one time, then it is logical to assume that God could allow suffering for a good purpose another time, and another time, and another time. An answer based in formal logic may not address the emotional question of an individual's situation. Still, it is reasonable to consider the possibility that even conditions that appear evil from a human perspective may be necessary to bring about a greater good.

There is another angle from which to view the suffering of Jesus. As one of the condemned men on the cross rightfully pointed out, Jesus was the Christ. That was more than just a theological point, though. Jesus had shown that He was able to perform many miracles, and many of these miracles helped relieve the suffering of people around Him. Jesus did not relieve His own suffering yet demonstrated many times that it was a good thing to alleviate the suffering of those around Him. If healing were not a good thing and therefore sin, Jesus would not have healed others. Therefore, Jesus' actions bring out a more nuanced picture of suffering. It can be good to relieve suffering, and it can be good to persevere through suffering. Suffering brings glory to God in every situation. Sometimes the removal of suffering was also used to bring glory to God, while other times, suffering, even to death, was used to magnify God.

One of the most poignant examples of healing bringing glory to God comes from John 9. A man had been blind from birth, and Jesus was asked why this man was blind. "And his disciples asked him, 'Rabbi, who sinned, this man or his parents, that he was born blind?'"[54] It is not that the disciples were trying to get Jesus to condemn this man. Rather, the disciples asked a genuine question about disability similar to the one in Job. They assumed if this man was blind, it must have been some type of judgment. Truth be told, this is a question that well-meaning Christians have whispered under their breath at times as well, even to this day.

Jesus turned the assumption around. "It was not that this man sinned, or his parents, but that the works of God might be displayed in him. We must work the works of him who sent me while it is day; night is coming, when no one can work. As long as I am in the world, I am the light of the world."[55] Jesus would later go to the cross for the same reason. He acted in obedience to the will of His Father, and He persevered for the glory of God.

---

54 John 9:2, ESV.

55 John 9:3-5, ESV.

It seems like Jesus is stating there is a higher purpose to the blind man's suffering, which is a challenging reality for many people who live with disabilities. It is hard to believe that sometimes excruciatingly difficult circumstances are given to certain people because God is meant to be glorified through them. Jesus almost directly answers the question from the book of Job. Job wanted to know why he was suffering, and God simply asserted that He was God and that should be enough. Jesus Christ gives a reason and raises another question. If God allows this disability because He wants to demonstrate His own glory, it needs to be asked whether or not God's glory is a sufficient justification. Is the glory of God important enough to justify allowing disability and evil generally?

There is no doubt that the glorification of God was the result of this particular miraculous healing. After the blind man went and washed the mud off his eyes that Jesus had put on him, the reaction of the people was immediate. "Neighbors and those who had seen him before as a beggar were saying, 'Is this not the man who used to sit and beg?' Some said, 'It is he.' Others said, 'No, but he is like him.' He kept saying, 'I am the man.' So they said to him, 'Then how were your eyes opened?'"[56] People had no idea that this kind of healing was possible. They thought this might be simply a man who looked a lot like the blind man they had known for years. The miraculous certainly does not happen every day; it is an exception to the general natural order by virtue of being a miracle. The world operates by cause and effect, and miracles are violations of that pattern. It was more reasonable for some in the crowd to conclude two people looked remarkably similar than to believe a miracle had happened.

The question then returns to whether or not glorifying God is sufficient justification for allowing disability. The apostle Paul writes in Colossians, "All things were created through him and for him."[57] If everything, including every person, was created for the glory of God, then the purposes of God would have predominance over all creation. We can conclude that following God's purpose is the highest possible calling of creation if that is what creation was initially designed to do. Therefore, to bring glory to God in any capacity is to fulfill that calling. If that means living life with a disability, then the justification would seem to be sufficient. In this particular situation, God did not allow a disability because He was evil or enjoyed seeing a specific man suffer. God allowed Him to be blind because it ultimately fulfilled the highest duty of creation.

Bailey also points out the importance of a long-term perspective when considering suffering in the context of the Gospels. "The New Testament links the suffering and hope of the believer with the suffering and resurrection of Jesus Christ. The interplay between the two shows that for neither of them is suffering meaningless. Meaning in suffering is best understood in light of the suffering of

---

56 John 9:8-10, ESV.

57 Colossians 1:16, ESV.

Jesus."[58] For the man who was born blind, his suffering had meaning as it brought glory to God. For Jesus Christ, His suffering had meaning because it brought glory to God. It is important to always keep this purpose in mind. Suffering for God's glory might not be generalizable, though. Every instance of suffering might not bring glory to God in this direct way and has not been shown to be logically necessary yet.

In John 5, Jesus healed a man who had not been able to walk for thirty-eight years. After the initial excitement over the healing had subsided, Jesus found the man in the temple and told him, "See, you are well! Sin no more, that nothing worse may happen to you."[59] The Bible does not specify how the man was injured originally. Perhaps it was some kind of moral sin that brought about his disability. However, that is an assumption that is not drawn out by the text.

Instead, Jesus explains that continuing to sin would ultimately lead to worse problems than his physical disability. Not being able to walk was a problem, and Jesus was able to help him with that one. Jesus told him to walk, and he did. However, Jesus did not tell him to go and enjoy his newfound ability even though that man was probably very excited to finally be able to have the mobility that he lacked for thirty-eight years. Jesus specifically told him not to sin anymore. He was supposed to stop violating the law of God. Again, that emphasizes the priorities that Jesus had when He was on earth. The problem with this man had never been his disability. Rather, his main problem was that he was a sinful man. The disability might have been something that he did not want to have, and previous statements regarding his efforts to be healed in the pool reinforce this perception.[60] However, Jesus reframes his perspective and tells him that no matter how bad he felt about his disability, he needs to stop sinning because that will lead to something much worse.

It is not that Jesus was trying to minimize the man's experience with disability. Jesus understood that his disability was difficult, and He delivered healing. Jesus met the physical need of that man, but He made sure that the man realized that his earthly body was not the most important thing in his life. It was more important that he understood that he was not supposed to sin. It was more important that he understood that following God is what fulfills humanity's highest calling. It is a question of priorities, and it is something that can easily be lost in day-to-day life. Physical needs seem to be the most immediate, but spiritual needs are truly more important.

Jesus maintained His commitment to a higher purpose throughout His ministry. The purposes of God are most important, and God did not tell everyone to

---

58   Mark L. Bailey, "A Biblical Theology of Suffering in the Gospels," in *Why, O God?: Suffering and Disability in the Bible and the Church*, eds. Larry J. Waters and Roy B. Zuck (Wheaton: Crossway, 2001), Kindle Edition

59   John 5:14, ESV.

60   John 5:7, ESV.

walk. God, however, did tell everyone to become disciples and make disciples.[61] The Great Commission is not conditioned on human ability. Even when Jesus was suspended on a cross and had most of His physical ability taken away, He was still able to continue acting in accordance with the will of God. When the blind man could not see, he could still be obedient to God's will and go to wash his eyes. Similarly, by not living a life of sin anymore, this man would have the ability to glorify God. He had that ability before he was healed, but Jesus used his healing as reinforcement. Since he was healed, he needed to remember that worse things could happen, like eternal separation from God.

Jesus suffered greatly during His time in ministry. As the Savior of the world, He took on the sin of every person and was obedient to the will of God. He went to the cross to experience that agony, and as a result of the literal suffering that He endured, He can identify with those who suffer. However, part of His ministry was also centered around relieving suffering. The blind man was given his vision back. The man who had not been able to walk for thirty-eight years was able to walk away. There were temporal benefits for these two men. Healing miracles allowed these men to live the remainder of the lives without the most evident manifestation of natural evil they experienced. They had abilities that they did not have previously. Having the ability to see or walk would have made life much easier, particularly in an age before very much adaptive technology.

However, all three of these examples brought glory to God. Jesus went to the cross for the glory of God. The blind man was healed for the glory of God. Jesus encouraged the man to make sure he did not sin anymore after being given the ability to walk. By living that life, he would also bring glory to God. Everything about the life of Jesus brought glory to God in one way or another. By extension, if followers of Jesus Christ are supposed to commit to demonstrating the glory of God on earth, then it seems to follow that living with a disability is part of the mission to bring glory to God. No one has an excuse for not becoming a disciple or making disciples.

D. The Pauline Epistles

As a leader in the early church, the apostle Paul understood what it was like to suffer persecution. He spent his life trying to spread the good news of Jesus Christ while traveling around the Mediterranean. His witness did not earn him very many friends among the religious establishment, and as a result, he had to endure many types of persecution. "We put no obstacle in anyone's way, so that no fault may be found with our ministry, but as servants of God we commend ourselves in every way: by great endurance, in afflictions, hardships, calamities, beatings, imprisonments, riots, labors, sleepless nights, hunger."[62] The book of Acts chronicles many specific instances of Paul's suffering, but it should suffice

---

61   Matthew 28:19, ESV.

62   2 Corinthians 6:3-5, ESV.

to say that Paul was not writing about suffering as an external observer. He understood what it was like to face adversity.

Paul himself likely had some type of physical disability. "Brothers, I entreat you, become as I am, for I also have become as you are. You did me no wrong. You know it was because of a bodily ailment that I preached the gospel to you at first, and though my condition was a trial to you, you did not scorn or despise me, but received me as an angel of God, as Christ Jesus."[63] Paul does not elaborate on his specific condition, so it is hard to tell precisely what Paul meant. Stanley Toussaint explains, "Speculation abounds as to what the thorn in the flesh was. Paul never identifies it. From Galatians 4:12–14 one may conclude that it was repulsive. This would constantly remind Paul to walk humbly before the Lord."[64] Of this disability, Jacober concludes, "Whatever this thorn was, it would certainly have taken him out of leadership by the Levitical standards. Yet, we know God used him mightily in his own time and for centuries beyond."[65] As a relevant side note, the fact that Paul was even willing to acknowledge his disability publicly shows the trust he had in God's provision. He trusted that God would use him even if any who judged from the exterior might doubt him, and God worked mightily through him. While Paul might have been speaking figuratively about some other struggle he experienced as his thorn, at the very least, Paul was suffering, and it very well might have been pain related to physical disability.

When Paul wrote his second letter to the Corinthians, he began by providing an update about how his missionary work was going.

> For we do not want you to be unaware, brothers, of the affliction we experienced in Asia. For we were so utterly burdened beyond our strength that we despaired of life itself. Indeed, we felt that we had received the sentence of death. But that was to make us rely not on ourselves but on God who raises the dead. He delivered us from such a deadly peril, and he will deliver us. On him we have set our hope that he will deliver us again.[66]

Job learned that he needed to trust God, and even if he did not understand everything that was going on, he had to understand that God was in control. David cried out to God for help during difficult times in his life, and he did that because he understood that he needed to place his hope in God. Jesus Christ was motivated by following the will of God. He perfectly obeyed the will of the Father, and trust is implicit in that kind of adherence.

---

63   Galatians 4:12-14, ESV.

64   Stanley D. Toussaint, "Suffering in Acts and the Pauline Epistles," in *Why, O God?: Suffering and Disability in the Bible and the Church*, eds. Larry J. Waters and Roy B. Zuck (Wheaton: Crossway, 2001), Kindle Edition.

65   Amy E. Jacober, *Redefining Perfect: The Interplay Between Theology and Disability* (Eugene, OR: Cascade Books, 2017), chap. 9, Kindle Edition.

66   2 Corinthians 1:8-10, ESV.

Paul encourages the believers in Corinth to recognize that his own power was inadequate to save him in Asia. Whether or not Paul himself had a disability is largely irrelevant in this passage because any human strength would not be enough. His only deliverance would come through the power of God, and that is exactly what happened. Their circumstances were mostly out of their hands, and they were despairing because they thought it was all over. However, Paul understood deliverance is never impossible for God.

Toussaint points out that "People learn about their own insufficiency and are left with only one alternative, namely, to trust in God."[67] Trusting, comfortably or not, is simply a reality for many people with disabilities. They might need help with almost all major life activities, and many things might be beyond their control. For example, nursing staff and personal care attendants receive trust from their clients. As tragic as it might be, though, those people are fallible. They will do things wrong now and then, and there will be disappointments. In those moments, even the people tasked with assisting with major life activities have not been helpful, and there is no one else to trust beyond God. God's grace needs to be sufficient because, without that, there are no answers left once everything on earth has failed.

Paul also recognizes the recurring Biblical theme that suffering can be used to bring glory to God. "If I must boast, I will boast of the things that show my weakness."[68] Suffering demonstrates human weakness, vulnerability, and the fact that people are not as invincible as they like to make themselves out to be. Etymologically, having a disability necessitates lacking a certain ability. Acknowledging the need for assistance is not meant to be dehumanizing but is a statement of reality. Having a disability, by definition, means that some major activity of daily life requires assistance. While some might lament weakness, Paul saw it as an opportunity to bring glory to God.

Because of his own temporary or permanent experience with a physical disability, Paul saw all of the good that could come from his own limitations.

So to keep me from becoming conceited because of the surpassing greatness of the revelations, a thorn was given me in the flesh, a messenger of Satan to harass me, to keep me from becoming conceited. Three times I pleaded with the Lord about this, that it should leave me. But he said to me, 'My grace is sufficient for you, for my power is made perfect in weakness.' Therefore I will boast all the more gladly of my weaknesses, so that the power of Christ may rest upon me.[69]

---

67 Stanley D. Toussaint, "Suffering in Acts and the Pauline Epistles," in *Why, O God?: Suffering and Disability in the Bible and the Church*, eds. Larry J. Waters and Roy B. Zuck (Wheaton: Crossway, 2001), Kindle Edition.

68 2 Corinthians 11:30, ESV.

69 2 Corinthians 12:7-9, ESV.

Paul had a vision he could not talk about, but it was something very special, and it might have been something that could have given him a sense of pride. However, he again mentions his affliction in Galatians. His condition was some kind of weakness that Paul did not want to have. He had been praying that God would remove it from him, but God did not remove his affliction. Instead, Paul learned through his experience that it was necessary to rely on the grace of God. Grace would be sufficient for him, and even though his affliction still bothered him, he understood that his weakness was actually a way to remember that God's power made the difference in his life.

Paul's words also speak to how God's power is made perfect in weakness. Does this imply that God's power is imperfect at all other times? Certainly not. Lacking omnipotence would go against the nature of God Himself. However, people try to rely on their own strength rather than God's. With complete trust in their own efforts, they find out there is no room left for trusting God, and they also discover that their best efforts are not enough. They want to hold on to some control, so they are only willing to trust God to a certain point. Paul is suggesting that God's applied power increases with increasing human weakness. Therefore, abandoning the need for complete independence and relying on the power of God seems counterintuitive but actually allows for the far greater power source to be glorified.

When God uses weakness to demonstrate His power, the problem of evil naturally comes up again. Did God purposely put difficult circumstances in people's life simply to bring glory to Himself? Isn't that at least somewhat egotistical? Many people would argue that that certainly seems unnecessary and unfair. If God is just, then why would He need to bring chaos into people's lives? Wouldn't there be an easier way to demonstrate His power?

A proper perspective on God's justice is essential. The ultimate question that the problem of evil suggests is whether or not it is more important to have a life that brings glory to God or a life that brings comfort. Therefore, when considering the problem of evil, it is important to remember again that it is possible for suffering to be used by God in the tradition of Swinburne. It can help bring people closer to Him, trust Him more fully, and bring glory to Him. In the process, the individual soul can develop further as well. There are multiple benefits to suffering in this context. Daniel R. Thomson tells the story of a man named Chuck Jones who was diagnosed with amyotrophic lateral sclerosis. His perspective seems to be in line with that of Paul. He did not seem to wrestle with the same questions as Job. Instead, he was concerned about living on mission, "Chuck was less concerned about the why of his diagnosis. Knowing his sovereign God, he wanted to know the what. What did God want to use this disease for in and through his life and the lives of others with the precious time he had left?"[70]

---

70   Daniel R. Thomson, "A Biblical Disability-Ministry Perspective," in *Why, O God?: Suffering and Disability in the Bible and the Church*, eds. Larry J. Waters and Roy B. Zuck (Wheaton: Crossway, 2001), Kindle Edition.

Even if the primary purpose of the entirety of existence, including disability, is to bring glory to God, it is not impossible to say that there are secondary purposes that are also good. One of those reasons could certainly be that, like Paul, these experiences allow for the betterment of our character. That will not only benefit us personally, but it will benefit the lives of those around us as well. Bringing glory to God will have benefits that trickle down from this principal purpose.

E. Revelation

Eschatology is a complicated field of study, and the book of Revelation is controversial in many circles because interpretations vary. Have many of the events described in the book already taken place? Are they currently happening right now? Are they still to come in the future? Mine is not a book about the end times, but the end of Revelation is mostly viewed consistently in Evangelical circles. In the new heaven and the new earth, because of the sacrifice that Jesus Christ made on the cross, the people of God have the opportunity to live with Him forever. There are many great promises made about this future, and they have implications for those who currently live with disabilities.

> And I heard a loud voice from the throne saying, "Behold, the dwelling place of God is with man. He will dwell with them, and they will be his people, and God himself will be with them as their God. He will wipe away every tear from their eyes, and death shall be no more, neither shall there be mourning, nor crying, nor pain anymore, for the former things have passed away."[71]

The eternal home of man with God will noticeably contain no suffering. There will be no more crying implying that there will be no more reason to cry. It is eternal, so there will be no more death. There will also be no more pain, which is significant because, for many people with certain disabilities, living with pain is a part of earthly reality. Going through even basic life activities can be an exercise in endurance and pain tolerance. Therefore, if there will be no more pain in the new heavens and the new earth, what happened?

First, it is wise to consider what resurrected bodies actually are. Using the chief passage in 1 Corinthians 15 concerning the difference between earthly and resurrection bodies, it should be clear that there is something fundamentally different about heaven and earth.

> As was the man of dust, so also are those who are of the dust, and as is the man of heaven, so also are those who are of heaven. Just as we have borne the image of the man of dust, we shall also bear the image of the man of heaven. I tell you this, brothers: flesh and blood cannot inherit the kingdom of God, nor does the perishable inherit the imperishable.[72]

---

71   Revelation 21:3-4, ESV.

72   1 Corinthians 15:48-50, ESV.

As Paul draws near the end of this epistle to the church in Corinth, he reminds them of their eventual victory. They are going to spend eternity with Jesus Christ. Paul speaks about bearing the image of the man of dust, which directly connects to creation when God created Adam out of dust.[73] Therefore, this is very clearly terrestrial imagery, and a contrast has been established between being on earth and being in heaven. There is some difference between these two kinds of bodies.

In the following sentence, there is a similar affirmation that flesh and blood are not capable of inheriting the kingdom of God, and there is a specific reference to the perishable not being able to inherit the imperishable. Paul's words again seem to speak to a literal understanding of these two different types of bodies. A body that is going to die would be unequipped to keep a person alive for eternity. God created an amazing machine when He created the human body. However, all humans are damaged by sin, and immortality is not an option anymore in the human body. Experientially, no one has lived forever on earth, and everyone's body has eventually given out at some point.

Transformation is necessary. There needs to be something different about heavenly bodies as opposed to earthly bodies. The glorified body will be eternal. "When the perishable puts on the imperishable, and the mortal puts on immortality, then shall come to pass the saying that is written: 'Death is swallowed up in victory. O death, where is your victory? O death, where is your sting?'"[74] Paul has not addressed disability yet, but there is no doubt that change will happen between heaven and earth.

Returning then to Revelation, it is clear that there will be no more pain. That implies no more physical suffering. The text also states that there will be no more crying and tears. That implies no more emotional suffering. That much is clear. However, the question reverts to whether or not disabilities inherently bring about suffering or if disabilities are simple characteristics of human existence in the same way that brown hair is a feature that is not inherently the cause of any suffering.

First, are certain disabilities in existence simply because of a genetic variation like brown hair? It is always dangerous to speculate, but if Adam and Eve hypothetically had not fallen, would it be possible that certain disabilities could have come about naturally in human history? It truly is impossible to know since there is no way to run an experiment on the DNA of the first human beings. Were harmful genetic mutations, for example, introduced into the human condition after the fall, or is there nothing wrong with genetic mutations, and they are simply variations in the original genetic blueprint of man as designed by God? Some genetic variations, like hair color, are harmless, so it is not hard to imagine them existing pre-fall. Other genetic variations, like those that cause disabilities,are more challenging. Whether or not these mutations and variations existed is simply impossible to know on earth. However, if genetic variations

---

73   Genesis 2:7, ESV.

74   1 Corinthians 15:54-55, ESV.

were inherent in people before the fall, then there is no reason to believe that those variations could not appear in resurrection bodies either.

Similarly, there is a question as to whether disability is inherently part of a person's identity or if a person's identity is something disability blankets but does not change. For example, a person might be Deaf. Being Deaf is a characteristic of a person who is unable to hear, but the question becomes whether or not identity is intertwined with disability. For example, if that person had not been Deaf, would there be any difference in who he or she is? Does disability define that person's identity, or is identity separate and a disability influences that on some level? Again, this is a question that is very difficult to answer because it is not as if history can be run through a computer program on an infinite loop. People are who they are, and there is no way to clarify to what extent disability is a part of identity and to what extent identity transcends the earthly difficulties brought about by disability.

At the same time, from my own experience, it is very hard for me to believe that I would have developed as a person in the same way that I did if I did not have my disability. I love sports. I could not play a competitive sport until I discovered power soccer as a freshman in college. Therefore, while I participated in sports as much as I could in various ways, like being a team manager, statistician, or sports reporter, my childhood was not centered around running to practice, working on my dribbling, or pursuing a puck around the rink.

I did not sit around in boredom, though. I did many things, and a lot of my passion got poured into my school work. My passion even extends to this day as I recently finished my Ph.D. Because I focused my energies in the direction of something I could do successfully, the person I became trended in that direction. My condition, spinal muscular atrophy, has nothing to do with intellectual ability, but my dedicated application of that intellectual ability into academics was framed by my physical disability and spiritual life. While this is speculation, I feel like I would have spent a lot more time on the baseball field than I spent hitting the books if I could do so. I don't know that for sure, but when I consider where my heart goes, I believe if I did not have my disability, most of who I am and who I consider myself to be would be different.

On the contrary, though, I may have been a terrible baseball player. Even if I could walk, I might not have been any good at sports and might have ended up hitting the books seriously anyway. I love what I am doing now, and maybe I would have realized that with or without the ability to physically compete. Again, this is a lot of speculation, and I will never know the answer to this thought exercise. That being said, I mention this personal reflection to try to emphasize that these questions regarding disability and identity are very hard, if not impossible, to separate from one another. It is an application of the classic question of nature versus nurture. While I certainly hope and expect to play a real game of baseball when I get to heaven and do not need this wheelchair anymore, there is certainly room to debate to what extent disability as an element of our identities will be preserved when we find ourselves in the presence of God. All that we can absolutely conclude from the Biblical testimony, disability or no, is that those who believe in Jesus Christ will dwell with Him, the fulfillment of all our desires, eternally in perfect joy.

Revelation presents difficult questions and important truths about disability and suffering. There will be no more physical or emotional suffering in eternity because there will be no more moral or natural evil. That much is clear, and that much is incredibly exciting for people who are used to living in a fallen world full of problems. The relationship between disability and suffering is slightly more problematic. Do disabilities necessarily bring about suffering? In some cases, the answer is absolutely yes. Many disabilities cause immense pain and suffering, so it would seem to make quite a bit of sense that those disabilities, or the painful elements of those disabilities, would not exist in eternity with God. However, not everyone with a disability would claim to be suffering necessarily. For example, a person who is blind might not believe he is suffering. Certainly, this person cannot see. There is no argument about that objective fact. However, it might not feel like suffering to the person who is blind, so the obvious question is how that relates to heaven.

Being blind might simply be a part of this person's identity and experience. If it does not cause any suffering, this characteristic of a person's identity might carry over into eternity. In the sense that there would be nothing problematic about having blue eyes in heaven, there might not be a problem with being blind. Suffering is a largely subjective term. It is also largely self-defined. For some, being blind might be the worst thing that could ever happen to them. Others do not see their blindness as a limitation or a significant challenge that causes suffering. It is possible for someone to say that there will be no more suffering in heaven but believe they will retain their disability because it is not anything that causes them suffering. It is simply an objective fact about them as a person.

However, since having a disability limits the full use of a God-given faculty and a blind person cannot take full advantage of the gift of sight, there is very good reason to believe that with a redeemed, heavenly body, those abilities will be fully available to everyone. Suggesting disability will not be present in heaven is not an attempt to demean anyone who lives with a disability but rather a recognition that disability itself very well might exist because of sin. God designed the human body to do certain things, and if it was created in that way, then the ability to do those things is good. In heaven, everything will be good. Therefore, for those of us who had never experienced the ability to do something like see, walk, or hear, we could have the ability to do those things which are good.

The elimination of disability does seem more probable than the continuation of disability into eternity. It seems God would want people to enjoy every gift He could give them, including all types of physical and intellectual ability, which are impaired in various ways here on earth. There is disagreement on the existence of disabilities in heaven within the Christian community. This discussion will continue in the next chapter. Still, it does seem to be the case that in Revelation, the removal of disability and the ability to embrace every good ability God originally put in Adam and Eve will be our reality for the rest of time.

F. Conclusion

Inspired by God, the Bible presents a consistent and undeniable picture of the dignity of those with disabilities. Any society that has sought to dehumanize individuals with disabilities has committed a great, objective evil. No matter how we view disability, there is no doubt from the Biblical testimony that individuals with disabilities are people created in the image of God and are therefore just as valuable as every other member of the human race. Hardwick writes, "When the church fails to assume the competence and value of those with disabilities, it surrenders to the same societal norms that disenfranchise the disabled."[75]

Beginning with what is assumed to be the first book of the Bible written, Job speaks to the problem of evil as one who did not understand everything God allowed to happen in his life. David did not understand why God was not coming to his aid or why he did not always receive an answer. The common thread between these two men is that they both trusted in God. Even though they did not understand everything and certainly wished that their circumstances were different, they did not abandon God.

Jesus Christ showed perfect adherence to the will of God through the Gospels, and through His life and death showed the world what it was like for an innocent victim to suffer for the sins of the world. Paul, who very well may have had a physical disability, encouraged his readers to rely on the power of God rather than their own strength. Revelation shows a world where suffering will be no more, and every tear will be dried. Interestingly, the New Testament speaks a lot more than the Old Testament about reconciling the existence of pain with the nature of God. While the Old Testament testimony focused on the question of evil, through the person of Jesus Christ, Paul's letters, and the vision of dwelling with God forever in Revelation, the New Testament paints a picture of purpose. While these answers do not necessarily address the exact contention made in the general formulation of the problem of evil, it begins to move towards its solution. Characteristics of God and how God works in the world suggest that evil in general or disability may not be meaningless as some contend.

Through these five Biblical examples, there is no wavering. They all affirm that God is in control and God is good. Disability can bring glory to God, and because that is the highest purpose of creation, it justifies the existence of any disability. Job, David, Jesus, and Paul experienced great adversity while fulfilling their purposes. However, there was meaning in those difficulties that each understood to varying degrees. The world is not without purpose, and just because someone experiences any type of difficulty does not mean that God doesn't care or God is not good.

The outline of five Biblical examples does not discuss the problem of evil to its conclusion, though. While it is reasonable to believe that there is meaning in

---

75 Lamar Hardwick, *Disability and the Church* (Downers Grove, IL: InterVarsity Press, 2021), 58, Kindle Edition.

some suffering, it is not logical to automatically conclude that there is meaning in all suffering. It is possible that if there is meaning in some suffering, there is meaning in all suffering. It is also possible for it to only mean just that: there is meaning in some suffering but not all suffering. Consequently, the argument needs to continue, and the next chapter will consider different perspectives on disability from the historic Christian tradition. Hopefully, building on the Biblical foundation established in this chapter and the outline of the various problems of evil in the previous chapter, a more specific answer to the problem of evil can be constructed.

Chapter 5

Church Tradition and Disability

The church has often been criticized as being hypocritical. Christians claim to believe in what the Bible says but often fail to live up to the standards they proclaim. Of course, Christians recognize that even with the forgiveness of God and the reconciliation of that relationship, sin is possible, and no one is perfect. The outside world does not always see Christians in that light, which certainly extends to discussions of disability.

There have been many theologies put forward about the relationship of disability to the problem of evil. As we saw in the previous chapter, even the disciples held to a theology of disability that taught that disability is a result of personal sin. They believed the man was born blind because either he sinned or his parents sinned. Jesus overturned their ideology, but that theology existed. As long as disability has existed, theologians have sought an answer as to why only certain people have to live with different physical and mental conditions.

Job came under similar criticism to the man who was born blind. His friends were convinced that he must have committed some type of sin. After all, everything had fallen apart in his life, and that simply should not happen to people who are following God authentically. Even though Job maintained his innocence and argued that he had no idea what he had done to bring about this series of events, his friends subscribed to a theology that taught suffering resulted from human decisions and human sinfulness. As readers of the story of Job, we know that the cause of Job's tragedy was not because of his sin. We can see the conversation between God and Satan where God gave Satan permission to do his worst, short of killing Job. However, his friends did not have this knowledge and therefore were embracing a theology that turned out to be incorrect.

Because there have been many problematic theological positions throughout history, it seems wise to look at an overview of the church's history and see how church tradition has handled disability. The best way to combat false ideas is to learn from some of the best minds that the church has ever produced. The letters of Paul and the teachings of the early church by extension have already been reviewed. Augustine, Thomas Aquinas, Martin Luther, John Calvin, Soren Kierkegaard, and Amos Yong will be examined to see how disability has been viewed throughout Christian history. While it is true that this is far from a comprehensive overview of everything Christians have ever said about disability, each one of these individuals has been chosen as a representative of different theological positions that will chronicle the development of different schools of thought within Christendom.

A. Augustine

Augustine understood that there was quite a bit of variation between people, and he wrote about that in *The City of God*. It is not that people with disabilities or any other variations were not human, but they were simply different. "Anyone who is born anywhere as a man (that is, as a rational and moral animal), no matter how unusual he may be to our bodily senses in shape, color, motion, sound, or in any natural power or part or quality, derives from the original and first-created man; and no believer will doubt this."[1] Augustine was not about to differentiate who was human and who was subhuman. Instead, all people descended from the race of Adam, no matter what variations might be present in their bodies, were still human. That would naturally include people with disabilities.

He continued to write about how very few people seemed to have perfect physicality. "It is, however, clear what constitutes the natural norm in the majority of cases and what, in itself, is a marvelous rarity."[2] In the larger context of this passage, Augustine speaks about conditions that some people described as "monstrous" (political correctness was different when Augustine was writing). He argued against the wrong belief that some people are ineligible to be classified as humans because of their differences. He made the simple observation that most people seem to have one type of disability or another. Some are more visible than others. Some impact major life activities more than others. However, no one is perfect.

A modern reading of Augustine may uncover certain ideas that remain popular while others might cause a degree of discomfort. On the one hand, Augustine undoubtedly put everyone on an even level before God. He understood that no one is perfect, so even though some people might have different challenges than other people, he rejected the assumption that most people are "normal" while people with disabilities are inferior. As has been previously stated in this book, any ideology that denies the humanity of people with disabilities is evil. Dehumanization is in direct contrast to the fact that all are created in the image of God.

However, the problem some readers would have with Augustine is that he is suggesting that all people are inferior, including people with disabilities. This line of theological reasoning has disturbed many people. Christians believe that all have sinned and fall short of the glory of God. Therefore, it is not that some people are overtly sinful; everyone is sinful. Applying this line of reasoning to

---

1   Augustine, "City of God, XVI.8 (707-10)," in *Disability in the Christian Tradition*, eds. Brian Brock and John Swinton (Grand Rapids: Wm. B. Eerdmans, 2012), 88, Kindle Edition.

2   Ibid.

the fact that no one is perfect physically, intellectually, or emotionally could be problematic in a modern context where acknowledging imperfection is seen as offensive. To affirm that disability is evidence of imperfection is an attack on the contemporary assumption that humans are naturally good.[3] Suggesting that someone may have an imperfection is, at best, foolish because with our modern cultural infatuation with denying the existence of objective truth, nothing can be perfect or imperfect. At worst, suggesting imperfection is seen as a moral judgment. If one does not affirm everything about someone as perfect, it is seen as intolerant, hateful, and offensive. Therefore, Augustine's suggestion that disability itself is not perfection and is one manifestation of the universal imperfection of the post-Eden world sounds hateful and intolerant to some.

Nevertheless, depravity is a fair portrayal of all humanity. Augustine does not single out disability as over and above any other evidence of the fallenness of the world. The existence of disability is no worse than the existence of anything else that may not be perfect about our world. Therefore, while some may be offended by Augustine's suggestion, it is not wise to view him as discriminatory. He affirms the fundamental Biblical truth that the existence of sin mars the world. Things are simply not going to be perfect all the time.

No one is inherently better or worse, but all people are in a temporary state of lacking some ability. Brian Brock summarized this truth by saying, "Augustine's theological norm for the human body rested upon judgments about ideal and real human capacities, but did not denigrate the lack of capacities he considered ideal. In most cases, however, he did assume that to lack some capacities was an inferior and mournful state."[4] Augustine's theology of disability remains influential throughout the history of the church.

B. Thomas Aquinas

Thomas Aquinas followed in the tradition of Augustine by understanding that no one is perfect. "For it is thus evident that by reason of the body the soul is hindered [as a consequence of original sin] from passing through things thrust in its path and from changing its location with as much ease as it does when separated from the body. In this way, also, it is kept from being able to have perfect use of its powers."[5] Because humans are inherently sinful people, everyone experiences limitations. No one's body can have "perfect use of its powers." Limitation in this context does not just include physical issues either. Instead, it encompasses the

---

3   An overview of this intellectual development can be found in Carl R. Trueman, *The Rise and Triumph of the Modern Self* (Wheaton: Crossway, 2020), Part II.

4   Brian Brock, "Augustine's Hierarchies of Human Wholeness and Their Healing," in *Disability in the Christian Tradition*, eds. Brian Brock and John Swinton (Grand Rapids: Wm. B. Eerdmans, 2012), 70, Kindle Edition.

5   Thomas Aquinas, "On Truth, 26.10," in *Disability in the Christian Tradition*, eds. Brian Brock and John Swinton (Grand Rapids: Wm. B. Eerdmans, 2012), 150, Kindle Edition.

entirety of the human experience. For any concerned about the Christian view being discriminatory, this provides further evidence that both Augustine and Aquinas viewed people with disabilities as people and did not single them out from any other group of people. They did, however, separate all of humanity from God due to human sinfulness. Therefore, while that may be offensive to our own myth of perfection, it is difficult to sustain the claim that believing disabilities are evidence of the fallenness of humanity is discriminatory against individuals with disabilities.

Aquinas expands on what goods are available to people on earth, and he does so without any exclusionary language about people with or without disabilities. "Such goods as these [necessities of the body] are nowise necessary for perfect Happiness, which consists in seeing God."[6] Emphasizing transcending earthly conditions is significant. There are good things on earth that are necessary to sustain life. However, Aquinas recognized that perfect happiness was not dependent on anything earthly. "That perfect Happiness which consists in seeing God will be either in the soul separated from the body, or in the soul united to the body then no longer animal but spiritual."[7] Aquinas' claim implies that simply by being human and having a soul, there is a way to achieve the perfect happiness from God. All can have a relationship with God. Miguel J. Romero writes, "According to Aquinas, no defect or disorder of the body can ever impair the principal operation and flourishing of the rational soul in its communication with God, which is an immaterial act of the soul."[8]

Aquinas is again in solid continuation with the work of Augustine. He affirms there is no advantage or disadvantage to having a disability. Everyone is the same before Jesus Christ, and as long as one is a member of the human race, he or she can communicate with God, the key to all human joy and happiness. There are no discriminatory filters keeping people with disabilities away from identification with humanity. Everyone is imperfect, and everyone has the potential to know God. People with disabilities have no greater separation from God than anyone else.

Aquinas took the common-sense approach of Augustine by appealing to equality before God. No matter what their physical, intellectual, or emotional condition on earth, all are separated from God, and all need God. However, Aquinas explicitly adds that a relationship with God is available to all people with a soul. In other words, anyone who is human can come closer to God. If all are the same before God and all are separated from God outside of the saving work of Jesus Christ, then the problem of evil as it relates to a disability

---

6   Thomas Aquinas, "ST, 1-2.4.7," in *Disability in the Christian Tradition*, eds. Brian Brock and John Swinton (Grand Rapids: Wm. B. Eerdmans, 2012), 131, Kindle Edition.

7   Ibid.

8   Miguel J. Romero, "Aquinas on the *corporis infirmitas*: Broken Flesh and the Grammar of Grace," in *Disability in the Christian Tradition*, eds. Brian Brock and John Swinton (Grand Rapids: Wm. B. Eerdmans, 2012), 107, Kindle Edition.

is no different than any other case of the problem of evil. The human equality inherent in the Christian worldview is vital. Affirming the human dignity of all actually differentiates Christianity from other worldviews such as utilitarianism that value people based on what they can contribute. Christianity views each individual person as an important part of humanity, no matter what society says.

C. Martin Luther

Martin Luther was the father of the Protestant Reformation, and his views on disability fall into a dichotomy. On the one hand, some of his statements appear incredibly offensive. For example, as recorded in *Table Talk*, he questioned whether a twelve-year-old boy with limited physical ability had a soul.

> I think he's simply a mass of flesh without a soul. Couldn't the devil have done this, inasmuch as he gives such shape to the body and mind even of those who have reason that in their obsession they hear, see, and feel nothing? The devil is himself their soul. The power of the devil is great when in this way he holds the minds of all men captive, but he doesn't dare give full vent to the power on account of the angels.[9]

Looking back on the teachings of Augustine and Aquinas, along with the Biblical testimony, it is clear that all people have souls. All people have souls because all people are created in the image of God.

Admittedly, it is difficult, even as a Protestant Christian, to come to the defense of Luther in this regard. His response may simply be evidence of a theologian who got something wrong in the face of a situation that he thought was the straightforward work of Satan. There was also a reasonably popular theological belief in his time that taught demons could swap themselves out for children, so it is possible to interpret Luther as believing that that is what had happened here.[10] If his impression were that this was a demon and not a child, his comments would make a great deal more sense. He was not dehumanizing a child from his perspective; he did not believe the child was there anymore due to malicious supernatural forces. While many people consider Luther's statement offensive, he becomes easier to read sympathetically and not automatically write off as discriminatory by understanding the historical context in which he said it. He was wrong theologically, but his intention does not appear as dark as it might seem on the surface.

---

9   Martin Luther, "LW 54: 396-97. 'Table Talk.' 1540. (WA TR 5: 8-9, No. 5207)," in *Disability in the Christian Tradition*, eds. Brian Brock and John Swinton (Grand Rapids: Wm. B. Eerdmans, 2012), 214, Kindle Edition.

10   M. Miles, "Martin Luther and Childhood Disability in 16th Century Germany: What did he write? What did he say?" *Independent Living Institute*, 2005, accessed December 28, 2020, https://www.independentliving.org/docs7/miles2005b.html.

In support of a more sympathetic interpretation of Luther, he affirms the humanity of people with disabilities. In his lectures on Genesis 1 through Genesis 5, Luther used an illustration about leprosy. "We still call a leprous human being a human being even though in his leprous flesh everything is almost dead and without sensation."[11] This section seems to pair quite nicely with the more sympathetic interpretation of the twelve-year-old boy. In that situation, he argued that the boy's body was essentially an animal with a different flesh. In this situation, he seems to be saying that even dead flesh remains human flesh. Luther seems inconsistent unless we interpret that the twelve-year-old boy's flesh was not really his own and was instead something evil put in his place. Again, theologically, this was not an unheard-of view in his time. It is crucial to view Luther in the culture and time where he was speaking.

In a sermon that Luther preached on the man born blind, he acknowledged the equality of all before Christ, much like Augustine and Aquinas. "For we are all blind and our light and our illumination comes solely from Christ, our good and faithful God."[12] He uses blindness as an illustration in this context, but he returns to the idea that everyone relies on Jesus Christ. Everyone includes people with disabilities and people without disabilities. In the same sermon, he speaks about those who become wrapped up in their earthly abilities. "Therefore let each one take heed, whether he be blessed with many or few of these gifts, that he by no means regard himself, but rather his neighbor, who does not possess the gift."[13] Luther believed that it was important for people to realize that everyone was separated from God. Just because someone had the ability to see, for example, did not mean that he should think any better of himself.

Luther turns the tendency to exalt one's self upside down. "Christ pays no attention to distinctions we make, for he bestows children and honor upon an old, unattractive woman just as readily as upon a beautiful woman, which is clearly illustrated in Rachel and Leah [Gen. 29: 21– 30: 24]. It makes no difference to him wherein he allows his work to appear."[14] Luther argues those who society might look down upon are possibly the people God might choose to work through. No one should assume who God is going to use; it is arrogant to do so. God works through everyone. Luther was more concerned that all have sinned and are separated from God. Secondary human characteristics are less important themes throughout this sermon.

---

11   Martin Luther, "LW 1:61. 'Lectures on Genesis Chapters 1– 5': 1: 26. 1535-1536. Translated by G.V. Schick. (WA 42: 45-46)," in *Disability in the Christian Tradition*, eds. Brian Brock and John Swinton (Grand Rapids: Wm. B. Eerdmans, 2012), 212, Kindle Edition.

12   Martin Luther, "LW 51: 35-43. 'Sermon on the Man Born Blind, John 9: 1-38.' 17 March 1518. Translated by J. W. Doberstein. (WA 1: 267-73)," in *Disability in the Christian Tradition*, eds. Brian Brock and John Swinton (Grand Rapids: Wm. B. Eerdmans, 2012), 200, Kindle Edition.

13   Ibid., 202.

14   bid., 202-203.

Luther argues that in John 9, there might be another layer of meaning to the healing of the blind man beyond the physical miracle. "The blind man was a sign of the blindness that lay hidden in our hearts."[15] Jesus Christ was not simply a miracle worker. He was able to defeat natural evil, and He was able to defeat moral evil. He came to create the bridge that fallen people needed to be reconciled to God. Therefore, while He did heal the blind man, He came to heal the hearts of all.

The dual meanings behind the healings performed by Jesus Christ are consistent with the many times Jesus spoke about His ultimate mission. Jesus was here to bring glory to God. It is probably safe to assume that Jesus enjoyed healing people as well. Presumably, He enjoyed seeing their reactions as their disabilities were taken away. However, He performed these miracles because He was following God's will and providing evidence that He was the Son of God. He was not simply performing miracles to remove physical, emotional, or intellectual barriers that people might experience. There was another purpose, so the dual meanings of Luther are supported by Jesus' actions as well.

Martin Luther was one of the most influential figures in the history of the church, and his views on disability are somewhat mixed. On the one hand, he seemed to dehumanize certain people with severe disabilities when read uncharitably. Perhaps Luther should be read uncharitably; I am not defending the infallibility of Martin Luther. However, when weighed against all of the other evidence from his work and the fact that there was a theological school that believed demons could physically trade places with children, reading Luther charitably does seem to make a greater deal of sense. This reconciliation squares him with the Biblical testimony, Augustine, and Aquinas in a way that makes more sense.

Luther strongly defended the equality of all people. Stefen Hauser summarizes the power of Luther's position quite well by pointing out that disability is not inherently any more problematic than any other facet of the human condition, "In the common life of all who are made equal by God's judgment, human beings are not judged on the basis of their abilities or disabilities."[16] From a Christian worldview, humanity's biggest problem is that all have sinned and fall short of the glory of God. Other problems occur throughout life, and none of the aforementioned theologians minimized the impact of suffering. However, they maintained the ultimate solution to all real or perceived problems in the world, including but not limited to disability, could only be found in Jesus Christ.

---

15   Martin Luther, "LW 51: 35-43. 'Sermon on the Man Born Blind, John 9: 1-38.' 17 March 1518. Translated by J. W. Doberstein. (WA 1: 267-73)," in *Disability in the Christian Tradition*, eds. Brian Brock and John Swinton (Grand Rapids: Wm. B. Eerdmans, 2012), 201, Kindle Edition.

16   Stefen Hauser, "The Human Condition as Seen from the Cross: Luther and Disability," in *Disability in the Christian Tradition*, eds. Brian Brock and John Swinton (Grand Rapids: Wm. B. Eerdmans, 2012), 197, Kindle Edition.

D. John Calvin

John Calvin understood that Jesus Christ was important for people with disabilities. "There are many people negligent in comforting themselves in God by his Word when they are afflicted with sickness, and so many die without the admonition or teaching which is more salutary for a man then than at any other time."[17] Again, this is a reaffirmation of the consistent testimony of prominent Christian leaders over the past two thousand years that the most serious problem with humanity is sin. Disability might be a problem, but it pales compared to the problem of sin in the world. Calvin suggests that it is vital for the pastor to visit and bring comfort from the Scripture when people are sick. In those potentially final moments of life, the most important thing for that person is understanding the saving work of Jesus Christ. Creamer draws attention to the fact that, "This demonstrates Calvin's interest in including all members of the community in the larger church, arguing that we must not deny access to Scripture (and, thus, access to the knowledge of God) based on physical condition or legal status."[18] She suggests that his insistence on the necessity of reciting the Catechism might be a problem for people with certain forms of intellectual disability.[19] Regardless, Calvin was dedicated to inclusivity. He was convinced that all people needed to come to Christ with disability and without, and it was the job of Christians to address the vital question of salvation.

Calvin also believed God has a purpose for suffering. His purpose might be different than people's purposes, but it does not mean that God is not good or is not in control. Even if God allows what appears to be evil, there could be an ultimately good reason for allowing suffering to take place. Similarly, he understood that Satan could afflict, so there may be three separate parties fighting for different positions in any situation.

> Satan is properly said, therefore, to act in the reprobate over whom he exercises his reign, that is, the reign of wickedness. God is also said to act in His own manner, in that Satan himself, since he is the instrument of God's wrath, bends himself hither and thither at His beck and command to execute His just judgments.[20]

Just because God allows Satan to act in certain situations does not make God morally suspect. Satan has his own temporary reign, and he is allowed to work

---

17   John Calvin, "Of the Visitation of the Sick," in *Disability in the Christian Tradition*, eds. Brian Brock and John Swinton (Grand Rapids: Wm. B. Eerdmans, 2012), 230, Kindle Edition.

18   Deborah Beth Creamer, "John Calvin and Disability," in *Disability in the Christian Tradition*, eds. Brian Brock and John Swinton (Grand Rapids: Wm. B. Eerdmans, 2012), 220, Kindle Edition.

19   Ibid., 220-221.

20   John Calvin, "God, Satan, and man active in the same event," in *Disability in the Christian Tradition*, eds. Brian Brock and John Swinton (Grand Rapids: Wm. B. Eerdmans, 2012), 238, Kindle Edition.

his wickedness. God, on the other hand, still has a plan. Even if there is evil, it does not mean that there cannot be good in a situation. Because God is in control, there will be something good that comes out of every situation. If a good God is ultimately in control, even in what He allows, He allows it for His purposes and His glory, which is good by definition.

Even with plenty of questions about the purposes of God, Calvin believed that the temporal would ultimately fade away. Once it does fade away, then eternity will remain, and that is much more important. "Whatever kind of tribulation presses upon us, we must ever look to this end: to accustom ourselves to contempt for the present life and to be aroused thereby to meditate upon the future life."[21] Calvin was writing for a Christian audience, and he suggests that even when life on earth seems unbearable, there is hope of eternal joy in heaven. All the pain will be worth it in the long run because Christians are even supposed to have contempt for the present life with its natural and moral evil. By realizing how corrupt the world is, Christians will consider their future life with God and the beautiful time that will be. If the world is too comfortable or has no difficulty, Calvin wondered how people would indeed be motivated to desire the world to come. "For this we must believe: that the mind is never seriously aroused to desire and ponder the life to come unless it be previously imbued with contempt for the present life."[22] In the Reformed understanding of the problem of evil, God's universe is a great story written by a great Author. Therefore, the narrative tension of being in the world drives Christians onward to the future world. Our story moves forward, and sometimes it takes a little bit of adversity to move us towards this ultimate goal. As in *The Hobbit*, the hero needs a little push out the front door to begin his adventure. It might appear unloving, but it also can be the beginning of the greatest thing that ever happened.

Some people might find Calvin's God mean-spirited if He specifically puts difficulties in the lives of people to draw them closer to Him or to desire eternity in heaven. However, from a Christian perspective, there is nothing better than dwelling with God forever. If there is truly nothing better than that, then anything that God does to draw people closer to His ultimate good would be justified. If a disability was necessary for a particular person to realize the need for surrendering to God, and if surrendering to God leads to salvation which is the greatest possible outcome, then the disability would be justifiable. Disability would consequently not be a problem or evil; it would be a necessary piece in God's plan to bring about the greatest good in the world. Of course, there is a debate about the nature of free will and predestination to be had, but Calvin did not see a problem with God allowing circumstances perceived to be evil if they brought people to the greater good.

---

21   John Calvin, "The vanity of this life," in *Disability in the Christian Tradition*, eds. Brian Brock and John Swinton (Grand Rapids: Wm. B. Eerdmans, 2012), 239, Kindle Edition.

22   Ibid., 240.

The primacy of salvation fits in with Calvin's previous emphasis on the importance of Jesus Christ for those who are suffering. For Calvin, everything comes back to the most important thing people could do on earth, preparing for eternity. No matter what happens on earth, it is more important for people to understand their need of salvation. All of life needs to be viewed through the lens of eternity. For understanding the problem of evil and disability then, Calvin brings the emphasis back to eternity. Eternity does not make suffering on earth any easier, but if being with God for all eternity is the best possible state, then there is no problem with going through any suffering on earth that will help move people towards that future.

E. Soren Kierkegaard

Suffering was not the ultimate problem in the world for Soren Kierkegaard. People indeed suffer, but he was much more concerned with salvation coming through the person of Jesus Christ. "You [who suffer] can still do — the highest thing of all. You can will to suffer all and thereby be committed to the Good. . . . Now you are indistinguishable from those whom you wish to be like — those that are committed to the Good. All are clothed alike, girded about the loins with truth, arrayed in the armor of righteousness and wearing the helmet of salvation!"[23] He agreed that there are problems in the world, and people need to live through those circumstances. However, before God, all are the same. All are sinners before God, and all have the option to follow and commit to God. If that is true, then even those who suffer should not be trying to be like people who do not suffer; Kierkegaard suggested that they try to be like those fully committed to the Good. Avoiding suffering is far from the chief end of life.

Considering Kierkegaard's commitment to following the Good, he would have no problem with the existence of disability. While he does not speak very much to the origin of disability and why God potentially allows disability to exist in the world, he raises the conversation to another level. He is more concerned about priorities. To Kierkegaard, there should not be any earthly pursuit that comes above the pursuit of God. Rather than complain about lacking ability, Kierkegaard focused the conversation on following God first and foremost. Once that priority is set, everything else fits into place.

Kierkegaard's perspective can be challenging because there is no person alive who has not dreamed of being like someone else. Growing up in the 1990s, anyone who ever touched a basketball wanted to "be like Mike" and achieve the superstar status of Michael Jordan. It is rather natural to desire or admire certain abilities that other people possess. However, Kierkegaard rightly recognized that emphasizing temporary things is not where the Christian needs to gravitate. "It

---

23   Soren Kierkegaard, "Those Whom Nature Has Wronged from Birth (Kierkegaard 1948, 160-69)," in *Disability in the Christian Tradition*, eds. Brian Brock and John Swinton (Grand Rapids: Wm. B. Eerdmans, 2012), 314, Kindle Edition.

is only too often the case that the sufferer shrinks from receiving the highest comfort, and the speaker is ashamed to offer the highest consolation."[24] People back away from receiving the comfort of God. They become wrapped up in temporary circumstances, and the comfort of God seems illusory. They assume nothing can help with their situation, so they hide away from God.

When faced with perceived suffering, most people try to provide comfort. A person without a disability might want to help someone with a disability focus on the importance of eternity with a genuine desire to comfort. Kierkegaard claimed that people are ashamed of doing so and does not have kind words for them. "Contrary to the truth, the consoling talk seeks to offer comfort by saying that the illness will soon be better — perhaps; and begs for a little patience. It coddles the sufferer a little, and says that by Sunday all will surely be well."[25] Kierkegaard again returns to the actual problem of humanity, which is separation from God. Therefore, it might seem easier to try to comfort people with disabilities, but that does not do them any good. Kierkegaard believed they need to follow God. He said that those who only offer comforting words without letting people know about the true comfort they can find with God are contrary to the truth.

Rejecting comforting words may not seem to provide a very good answer to the pastoral problem of evil. There are times when it seems to be good and right to weep with those who weep. There are times just to be there and support, perhaps without saying or doing anything. Anyone who has ever tried to console someone who just lost a loved one understands this. Kierkegaard's solution may seem insufficient in these situations. However, it is worth considering that he never says not to comfort. Rather, he redirects the conversation to a different kind of comfort than that person might be expecting. He does not say to be brash or cold but rather to try to transition from sorrow to a source of comfort that will never disappoint.

Modern society focuses on the temporary prescribing of medications to fix temporal problems. Therefore, when talking about disability, the obvious way to address the problem for many in the secular world is to create a more accommodating world. If there are more ramps, more braille signs, and a more understanding populace, disability will become less of a problem across the board. On some level, that is true. Recall back to the definition of disability and the idea that environmental or attitudinal barriers can exacerbate disability. However, from a Christian worldview, accessing a specific building has absolutely no eternal consequence. Jesus Christ is the answer to all problems in the world, so Kierkegaard kept his focus on this reality. It is not that he opposes comfort, but he realizes that the good news of Jesus Christ and encouraging the pursuit of God needs to be the priority.

---

24 Soren Kierkegaard, "Those Whom Nature Has Wronged from Birth (Kierkegaard 1948, 160-69)," in *Disability in the Christian Tradition*, eds. Brian Brock and John Swinton (Grand Rapids: Wm. B. Eerdmans, 2012), 314, Kindle Edition.

25 Ibid., 314-315.

Kierkegaard does not suggest that disability is something that inherently needs to be fixed. Christopher Craig Brittain points out that, "His references to illness and weakness are not primarily comments on individuals' physical abilities and health, but on their relationship to sin — that is, their relationship to God, fellow human beings, and especially their own inward relation to themselves."[26] If all are equal before God, then disability is a fact of life for certain people. Kierkegaard speaks directly against critics like the friends of Job, who argue that disability is a punishment for specific sins. He focused on the higher calling of Jesus Christ, which is the most important pursuit a person could have. "The real reason that men are offended by Christianity is that it is too high, because its goal is not man's goal, because it wants to make man into something so extraordinary that he cannot grasp the thought."[27]

For the Christian apologist, the work of Soren Kierkegaard provides a framework for recognizing that, first of all, disability is a fact of life. There are treatments, medications, and cures for many conditions in the world, but for other people, outside of divine intervention, healing is simply not going to happen. The world is driven by the faith that people place in medicine. If medical professionals have not figured out a way to solve a certain problem, more research must be done to stop perceived suffering. Kierkegaard would argue that worrying exclusively about the physical is missing the point entirely. Like the other theologians examined in this chapter, he understood that humanity needed to deal with its separation from God first. Without reconciling that relationship, everything else was for naught.

F. Amos Yong

Amos Yong takes a unique view of and writes, "A disability perspective would insist that some impairments are so identity-constitutive that their removal would involve the obliteration of the person as well."[28] He believes that several disabilities do not bring about any physical suffering but rather bring about a socially constructed problem that then turns into suffering. "In this normate theological construct, then, disability is a postlapsarian and accidental intrusion into the created order which the eschatological transformation will eliminate once and for all, thus simultaneously comforting the afflicted . . . and making

---

26   Christopher Craig Brittain, "Between Necessity and Possibility: Kierkegaard and the Abilities and Disabilities of Subjectivity," in *Disability in the Christian Tradition*, eds. Brian Brock and John Swinton (Grand Rapids: Wm. B. Eerdmans, 2012), 290, Kindle Edition.

27   Soren Kierkegaard, "Sin as the Disability (Kierkegaard 1980, 22, 81-83, 85)," in *Disability in the Christian Tradition*, eds. Brian Brock and John Swinton (Grand Rapids: Wm. B. Eerdmans, 2012), 312, Kindle Edition.

28   Amos Yong, *The Bible, Disability, and the Church: A New Vision of the People of God* (Grand Rapids: Wm. B Eerdmans, 2011), chap. 5, pt. 2, Kindle Edition.

'them' exactly like 'us.'"[29]

Yong emphasizes a crucial point that is far too often overlooked. There is an element of disability that is socially constructed. Perhaps he pays attention to the socially constructed aspect of disability because he is a modern theologian and lives when people are more sensitive to the effect of society on the individual. Discussions of social constructions would simply not have taken place in centuries past as it is a very modern creation of, largely, the academy. The effects of disability can be exacerbated by societies that do not understand or are unwilling to help make accommodations for people to perform major life activities. However, claiming disability is entirely socially constructed is problematic because, even though there is an element of living with a disability that is socially constructed, the disability still exists medically outside of society's response to it. If disability was entirely socially constructed, then, by taking that concept to its logical conclusion, once everywhere in the world was wheelchair accessible, not being able to walk would no longer be a disability. Even with all of the ramps and elevators in the world, a person who uses a wheelchair still has a disability because he or she lacks the ability to walk. That disability might not be an obstacle, but by the definition of disability used throughout this work, it still prevents people from performing the major life activity of walking. Similarly, for someone who is blind, even with all of the accommodations made to help him or her participate in every area of society, the simple fact of the matter is that he or she still cannot see.

Yong's commitment to the social construction of disability also influences his eschatological views. He holds the belief that certain types of disability will be present in heaven. Yong explains why it is so important for him to understand disability and redeemed heavenly bodies in this way,

> Eschatological images without people with disabilities abilities effectively translate into churches —harbingers of the coming reign of God — without such people, either. We have unconsciously constructed communities of faith heralding the new heavens and the new earth in which the sick can expect to be healed and the disabled can receive their cures.[30]

He worries that creating a culture where disabilities are viewed as a result of the fall creates a society where people with disabilities are viewed as exceedingly sinful. His concern harkens back to the question the apostles asked Jesus Christ about the man born blind. They wondered if it was for his own sin or his parents' sin that he was born lacking the ability to see. Yong does not want to bring that type of ideology into the church today, and his purpose is noble. It is good to have a church that is inclusive regardless of disability. However, the possibility of some people believing disabilities are caused by sin draws him to a different eschatological position which allows disabilities in heaven.

---

29   Amos Yong, *The Bible, Disability, and the Church: A New Vision of the People of God* (Grand Rapids: Wm. B Eerdmans, 2011), chap. 5, pt. 2, Kindle Edition.

30   Ibid.

Yong considers disability a central part of identity that needs to be retained in eternity. Recall that he believes removing certain disabilities that are not causing "suffering" would strip a person of his or her identity. He believes that disability is part of the original genetic variation embedded in humanity rather than a consequence of the fall. "This [prejudice in interpretation] in turn underscores the normate theological hermeneutic which defines disabilities solely in terms of sin and the Fall rather than in terms of the bodily differentiation originally blessed in the creation."[31] Therefore, the ultimate question comes back to what the transformed body will be and what characteristics will define that eternal existence.

In the earlier section about Revelation, the issues surrounding the removal of suffering in eternity have been discussed. The Biblical testimony seems to suggest the absence of any suffering or tears and the desire of God for His creation to have every good gift. In that sense, the evidence would seem to lean away from the interpretation that Yong has proposed. He also suggests that disabilities are identity-constructive. Lives are indeed partially formed by nurture. The situation that I find myself in will help develop my identity. However, it is a major assumption to think that my identity now is actually my true identity. What if my true identity actually never developed the way it should have because of living with a disability? Disability is partially identity-constructive, but it is worth asking if disability constructed my true identity or an identity shaped by the reality where I exist right now. What if my identity would have been entirely different but was altered to its current state by my circumstances, and any change that will take place in heaven will actually bring it back to its true state?

Questions of identity do not just challenge people with disabilities. We all will be ourselves in heaven, but the selves that we know as ourselves on earth are twisted by sin. It is worth asking whether any of us, with a disability or not, know our truest selves. As a result, it very well might be the case that many elements of our lives that are identity-constructive on earth get stripped away. We will still be ourselves, but with reoriented appetites and desires, we are all going to be different. Ultimately, that is a good thing, moving us to the reconciliation we have all been seeking.

Yong's point is certainly well taken, and it is vital that the church does not become a place where disability is disfavored. As Hardwick writes, "Diversity, then, is more than desegregation; diversity is rooted in full integration. The difference between the two is as distinct as merely being allowed in versus being whole-heartedly included."[32] Yong and Hardwick's concern has been addressed by each theologian already mentioned. The historic church has consistently affirmed the humanity of all people with and without disabilities. However, it is unclear

---

31 Amos Yong, *The Bible, Disability, and the Church: A New Vision of the People of God* (Grand Rapids: Wm. B Eerdmans, 2011), chap. 5, pt. 2, Kindle Edition.

32 Lamar Hardwick, *Disability and the Church* (Downers Grove, IL: InterVarsity Press, 2021), 38, Kindle Edition.

whether Yong's interpretation should extend to a determinant of eschatology. It is objectively evil when churches discriminate against individuals with disabilities, but abuses should be addressed directly rather than theology altered. There are better ways to encourage inclusivity than changing to a theology that is more Biblically questionable. It does not seem to be entirely consistent with the Biblical testimony, specifically Revelation.

Nevertheless, there is much to learn from the work of Yong. He emphasizes the importance of society accommodating for individuals with disabilities and the shared humanity of all people. He argues for the dignity of those with disabilities. He does not want to see the church become a place where people with disabilities are written off as broken or somehow more sinful by having a disability. In fact, I had the privilege of appearing on the radio show with a friend where I made arguments very similar to Yong's about the need for congregations that are welcoming to people with disabilities.[33] Access and dignity issues need to be talked about.

G. Conclusion

Answering the problem of evil is a question of worldview, and it extends beyond Augustine, Thomas Aquinas, Martin Luther, John Calvin, Soren Kierkegaard, and Amos Yong. They were and are Christian men who knew God was real. They knew that they had put their faith in the Ruler of the universe, and they knew that God had certain characteristics. Therefore, the question was not whether God would allow disability or other forms of suffering in the world. The evidence was clear. These things do exist, so the question was then trying to figure out how that relationship was defined. Each of these men had slightly different approaches to answering the problem of evil. If God is perfectly good, all-powerful, and all-knowing, how could He allow evil?

Augustine spoke to the importance of affirming the humanity of all. No matter what type of disability a person experienced, Augustine was correct in pointing out that disability did not take away an individual's humanity. Granted, he used a broader definition of disability than what is being affirmed in this book, but he still took a very strong position towards affirming dignity. Thomas Aquinas continued Augustine's tradition by recognizing that while disability might be perceived as a problem by some people, the greatest problem with humanity is the sin has separated everyone from a relationship with God, and that relationship needs repair for anyone with or without disabilities. Martin Luther was committed to the idea that God can work through everyone. Amos Yong similarly emphasized that there is a place for all in the family of Christ, and churches need to be welcoming places. These theologians fit into a pattern of continuation. Augustine pointed out the humanity, Aquinas emphasized the

---

33   "Wrath and Grace Radio | Disabilities and the Church," *YouTube*, March 22, 2020, accessed April 25, 2021, https://www.youtube.com/watch?v=g9av0QyPrzU.

equality, and Martin Luther brought attention to the potential of all to bring glory to God. Yong reminds the church that society and church communities are the places that allow that potential to come into existence.

Calvin and Kierkegaard called attention to the higher priorities of humanity. Calvin understood that even in cases of severe disability, God could have a good purpose. If God does have a higher purpose, then any difficulties are justified because it is better to be in the will of God than anywhere else for now and for eternity. Kierkegaard had a similar desire to pursue God. He argued that words of comfort are not worth very much without a presentation of the gospel. He realized that the gospel is truly the only real hope and comfort that anyone has. Again, like Calvin, he understood the long-term implications of following God. As a question of priorities, both Calvin and Kierkegaard realized that the higher calling of God was more important than temporary comfort or temporary ability.

By and large, these six theologians brought a consistent testimony regarding the traditional Christian position on disability. Even though they did not specifically address the problem of evil in the way discussed earlier in this book, they provide insight into how the reality of disability is handled in practical terms. Theirs is a much more pastoral approach to solving the problem of evil than the theoretical approaches of the aforementioned apologists. Parents who are raising their first child with a disability will want to hear that God loves their child as much as any other child. They might want to listen to the teachings of Aquinas, for example. His approach will be much more accessible and approachable than a philosophical discussion of the problem of evil and all of the possible worlds that God might have created. Both approaches rely on the same doctrinal underpinnings, but one communicates in a way that makes more sense to those who might not be trained in formal logic.

Nevertheless, the problem of evil still needs to be faced head-on. Each of these six theologians adds a great deal of value and contributes an important perspective to discussing the problem of evil and disability, but all of these arguments now require synthesis. Hume and Mackie want to know how God can be everything Christians say He is and yet still allow evil in the world. To many, the presence of disability appears to be evidence of that evil. People make decisions that harm other people, and even our genetic code is not protected from mutations and other flaws that create very real problems in individual lives. Therefore, it is now time to apply everything that has been gleaned from studying different perspectives on the problem of evil, Biblical perspectives on disability, and the church's tradition on disability to come to a final resolution about understanding disability in a universe created and sustained by an all-powerful, all-knowing, all-good God.

Chapter 6

Disability and the Problem of Evil

Although it might seem like a significant portion of this book has been dedicated to background information, it is essential to establish a foundation for disability and the problem of evil before exploring how they interact. Recall that at the beginning of this exploration, the problem of evil as it relates to disability asks why God allows disability and does not heal everyone immediately. Many people argue that God cannot be good because God allows people to get injured in automobile accidents. After being hit by a drunk driver, they might spend the rest of their lives dealing with the repercussions of a spinal cord injury. The secular world asks why God does not heal amputees. If God is all-good, all-powerful, and all-knowing, why does God not make an arm or leg grow back?

After evaluating the Biblical testimony, church history, and contemporary approaches to solving the problem of evil, it is finally appropriate to begin directly tackling these questions. First of all, there will be a discussion about reformulating the problem of evil, specifically through the lens of disability. Second, this chapter will move into putting together a proper defense of why God allows disability. Keep in mind that this will not be a theodicy. As the author, I would not presume to absolutely know the mind of God. Rather, in the spirit of Plantinga's free will defense, the purpose of my approach will be to show why the existence of disability does not disprove the existence of God. Since the popular question asks why God does not always heal people with disabilities or allows things to happen that cause suffering, the implicit accusation is that such a God must not exist. Therefore, if the defense proposed by this chapter can show that it is possible for God to simultaneously exist with the existence of specifically disabilities, it will have served its purpose and successfully refuted the argument that disability and suffering necessarily disprove the existence of God.

It should also be mentioned that when I provide this defense, I am not personally Reformed. Therefore, while I did include the Reformed position on solving the problem of evil in the appropriate chapter and included Reformed theologians in my brief survey of traditional church teaching on disability, I will not be operating from that perspective in this chapter. I could write a defense related to my reasons for not doing so, but that would not suit the purpose of this book and would take far too much time and focus away from the topic of disability. I will leave the project to an individual who is of the Reformed persuasion to consider disability and the problem of evil from their own perspective, which will probably be better than any arguments I could try to represent for them.

A. Reformulating the Problem of Evil

Recall that the problem of evil has a relatively basic structure as formulated by J. L. Mackie. "In its simplest form, the problem is this: God is omnipotent; God is wholly good; and yet evil exists. There seems to be some contradiction between these three propositions, so that if any two of them were true the third would be false."[1] For many people who believe that the existence of disability is incompatible with the existence of an all-powerful, fully good God, they are essentially substituting disability for evil. They are saying that God is omnipotent; God is wholly good; and yet disability exists.

Many disability rights advocates would disapprove of this substitution because the obvious implication is that disability is evil. Many would argue that this is insulting their identities as individuals with disabilities. For instance, Patricia Bruce, in writing about how some may find offense in the fact that Jesus was "fixing people" with disabilities when He brought healing, explains,

> This is a serious matter. In our society, anything that serves to undermine the value of people with disabilities has far-reaching implications, especially in a context where genetic testing, which can prevent many disabilities, also raises the question of whether this implies a negative evaluation of the lives of people with disabilities.[2]

She argues that she does not believe this was Jesus' intention, but she has a genuine concern for the perception of the disability community.

The reality is, however, that some people do view their own disabilities as evil. Therefore, they feel comfortable making this substitution. In their own worldview, disabilities or the disabilities of those around them are conditions that are undeniably wrong with the world, and just like any other problem of evil, it needs to be answered for and justified. If there were absolutely nothing wrong with disability, it would not be worth asking why God does not heal everyone. If there was nothing wrong with it, then being healed or not healed would be functionally equivalent.

The Christian worldview takes a more nuanced approach to this topic than just equating disability and evil. Yes, there is something about disability that seems to go away in eternity, so it would be easy to write off all disability as necessarily evil. As shown by the testimony in Revelation, the Bible teaches that there will be no more suffering for those who will dwell in the house of the Lord forever. However, that raises the question as to whether or not every disability necessarily involves suffering. Many members of the Deaf community do not consider being

---

1   J. L. Mackie, "Evil and Omnipotence," *Mind* 64, No. 254 (April 1955): 200, accessed March 5, 2016, http://www.jstor.org/stable/2251467.

2   Patricia Bruce, "Constructions of Disability (Ancient and Modern): The Impact of Religious Beliefs on the Experience of Disability," *Neotestamentica* 44, no. 2 (2010): 272, accessed November 26, 2020, http://www.jstor.org/stable/43048759.

Deaf a disability. They certainly do not believe they are suffering because it is simply a part of who they are. Similarly, a person who was never able to walk might not consider lacking the ability to walk to be suffering. It simply is the way reality is for that person, and suffering might not seem to apply in that case. Therefore, Revelation speaking about no more pain and no more tears simply might not seem relevant to some people who have disabilities.

It might then be easy to conclude that Yong's aforementioned argument is valid, particularly on this point. Disability is not inherently evil and therefore might exist in eternity future in the presence of God. However, the problem with Yong's idea is that Jesus performed miracles while He was on earth. Those who were blind were able to see. Those who had never been able to walk were able to walk. Jesus was restoring abilities that these people did not have yet were in the original design of humanity. It would seem odd for Jesus to waste His time fixing something if it did not need to be fixed. For example, God did design eyes to have the ability to see. Feet are generally created to be walked on. Therefore, when Jesus was restoring these abilities to people, it seems to be the case that there is something about disability that is inherently in need of repair. At any rate, healing was valuable enough for Jesus to spend time doing. Healing was also consistent with His overall mission of bringing glory to God in whatever He was doing.

Kierkegaard, in particular, mentioned that all of humanity requires repair. Because of the fallen world, evil caused damage in every area. If that is the case, then why would the human condition be any different? As Luther pointed out, different people have different gifts. If that is true, then there is a range of ability and disability, but it all falls under the entire umbrella of imperfection because the world is not an ideal place. Because sin has entered the world, subsequent challenges might manifest themselves in different ways for different people. Some people are more intelligent, while others are less intelligent. Some people are Olympic athletes, while others have to rely on machines to breathe. In a Christian worldview, none of them are perfect. Theologians often talk about perfection in moral terms. However, considering physical perfection, even elite athletes atrophy over time. Even the strongest see their physical condition deteriorate. Many brilliant people develop Alzheimer's or dementia later in life. Therefore, perfection can be spoken of in moral terms, but it is also important to consider in terms of the human body.

From a secular worldview, it is easy to see how survival of the fittest would favor those who appear to be closer to whatever the ideal human being is. The practice of eugenics is evidence of Darwinism applied to societies.[3] However, the Christian worldview teaches there is no perfect human outside of Jesus Christ, so when speaking about evil and then trying to specifically define what this means for people with disabilities, identifying evil with people with disabilities is to

---

3   Zak Schmoll, "A Silent Genocide: Disability and the Ongoing Consequences of Social Darwinism," in *An Unexpected Journal: Image Bearers* 4, no. 1 (Spring 2021), March 10, 2021, accessed April 24, 2021, https://anunexpectedjournal.com/a-silent-genocide-disability-and-the-ongoing-consequences-of-social-darwinism/.

identify them with being human. As much as we might decry charges against our self-proclaimed perfection, the history of mankind bears out the reality that everyone with any level of ability is separated from God on account of sin. There is no magic formula of ability and disability that makes someone more holy. All have sinned and fall short of the glory of God. Therefore, the existence of evil ironically affirms an element of our shared humanity in this world. All experience moral and natural evil.

The secular definitions of disability, like the ones presented in this book, are not entirely satisfactory. These definitions claim that disability is not something that everyone has. Certainly, everyone does have a sin nature, though, so all people are necessarily under that umbrella. However, not everyone qualifies for any specific definition of disability. All people with disabilities are fallen humans, but not all fallen humans are people with disabilities. Therefore, even though taking the perspective of these theologians helps refine the statement of the problem of evil related to disability, there are still problems with that compilation.

Perhaps disabilities are the consequence of the fall. Although Yong would argue that disabilities are part of the natural diversity of genetics in humanity, when considering that eyes are organs designed to see, muscles are designed to move, and ears are designed to hear, it would seem strange to say that in a perfect world God would have designed things that did not work for their intended purpose. After introducing the consequences of sin, all creation felt the repercussions, and the human body was no different. Even very early in the Old Testament, readers meet Moses with a speech impediment.[4] Even though disability is nothing new, disability does not seem to have been present in the Garden of Eden or in Adam and Eve. Assuming that disability is part of human natural genetic variation also disregards disability caused by the evil actions of others which did not happen before the fall.

As pointed out by Jesus Christ Himself, disability is not necessarily a consequence of sin in the lives of an individual or his or her parents. Instead, Jesus points out that it possible for disability to be something that brings glory to God. In John 9, a man was healed, and God was glorified due to that miracle. Therefore, it is not a case of this man doing anything particularly evil in his teenage years that brought about divine judgment. There is a differentiation between disability being a consequence of living in an evil world or a consequence of a particular person being particularly evil or sinful.

Therefore, it does not seem responsible to simply substitute disability into the traditional formula for the problem of evil. Disability is a consequence of evil, but it does not seem to be equivalent to evil itself. Consider Job as an example. He suffered greatly because there was evil in the world. If Satan had not been in

---

4   Exodus 4:10, ESV.

existence, Job's testing would have never taken place. Job was not perfect, so he contributed to the fact that the world was not a perfect place, but his disability was not the consequence of his personal evil. Job was not like Sodom and Gomorrah. Those cities committed specific crimes that brought judgment; Job was simply living in a world that was corrupted by human abuse of free will.

Therefore, it is not valid to formulate the problem of evil concerning disability as, "God is omnipotent; God is wholly good; and yet disability exists." Disability is a consequence of moral or natural evil in the world. Everything does not function the way that it was designed because of evil in the world. While all humans do bear responsibility for contributing to the problem of evil, disability does not seem to be, based on the Biblical testimony, specific punishment for people who have been particularly evil or sinful. A great many disabilities are also the consequence of natural evil.

If that is true, then reformulating the problem of evil would still affirm the first two premises. God is omnipotent, and God is wholly good. Those are still fundamental truths affirmed by the Christian worldview. However, the conclusion regarding evil existing needs to be modified because God allows consequences of evil. Even if disability itself is not evil, God could have intervened and made the human genetic code unaffected by sin nature. God could have made it so that people do not have snowboarding accidents that leave them paralyzed. However, God did not do that. He allows human free will to play out, and the consequences of living in a fallen world impact everyone every day. As originally discussed at the beginning of this book, many types of evil wreak havoc, but because God has allowed humanity to have free will in a world governed by cause and effect, if there is sin, there will be consequences from that sin. Reformed readers will disagree with the origin point of evil being rooted in free will, but, as previously stated, debating the relative merits of Reformed theology expands beyond the bounds of this particular book.

It does not seem to be the case that disability was in the original design of the world. If everything is good, then everything would function as designed, including the human body. Affirming properly functioning bodies is not meant to diminish people who have disabilities. Instead, it is a recognition that the fall manifests itself in various ways in all humans; some ways are simply more visible than others. Whether discussing a chemical imbalance or extraordinarily weak muscles, a disability is another piece of evidence that not everything functions as it was designed to function. Disability is actually is a strong affirmation of the humanity of people with disabilities. All humans are fallen, and disability is an unambiguous affirmation of the challenges that have developed in the world because of humanity's original abuse of its free will and continuing spiral down that path.

Considering disability as a consequence of evil also satisfies the problem of labeling disability as a punishment for individual sin. A person has no control over his or her genetic code. A person has no control when a drunk driver hits his or her vehicle. However, bad things indeed happen in the world, and they occasionally happen to people who have done nothing specific to bring evil upon themselves besides being a part of the world. No one is innocent of sin; all have sinned. However, for the purposes of exploring disability, it is much more appropriate to consider that there is nothing extraordinarily evil about people with disabilities; rather, they simply have a more obvious manifestation of the consequences of evil in the world. Without connecting disability to personal evil, it is possible to consider disability being caused by natural evil as well. If disability was necessarily connected to personal evil, there would be no way to explain the role that natural evil plays in disability. If disability equates to evil itself, the connection to personal evil appears more necessary, a position that this book has thoroughly refuted.

When considering the three approaches to addressing the problem of evil, two of them would affirm viewing disability as a consequence of evil. The impact of consequences is implicit in the free will defense; people feel the consequences of wrong decisions made by free agents. Similarly, a soul-making theodicy would affirm that virtues can be developed by allowing a certain amount of evil in the world. Reformed believers would dispute calling disability a consequence of evil choices because it relies on decisions made by free agents, but, again, that debate is not the primary focus of this chapter and this book. Reformulating the problem of evil to suggest that disability is not equal to evil but rather a consequence of evil provides clarification as well as correction. It affirms the humanity and value of people with disabilities while recognizing the existence of disability in the world and putting it in its proper place.

B. Addressing the Redefined Problem of Evil

The problem of evil has been reformulated as follows for the purposes of this discussion, "God is omnipotent; God is wholly good; and yet consequences of evil (like disability) exist." Therefore, many of the same questions that the traditional problem of evil brings about arise again. First of all, why does God not heal everyone immediately? After all, God has the power to do whatever He wants if He is omnipotent. God could, and did, make blind people see and deaf people hear.[5] People were able to walk after Jesus healed them. Therefore, why does this not happen universally?

The first thing to consider is that if disability is a consequence of living in a fallen world, then the world is fallen for a reason. The free will defense addresses this very well. If God allows people the freedom to choose whether or not they will follow Him, then that choice would not be free if God began restricting that freedom when people made bad choices. It would not be true freedom if God did not allow bad consequences to happen.

---

5   For more detail on miracle claims, see Craig S. Keener, *Miracles: The Credibility of the New Testament* (Grand Rapids: Baker Academic, 2011).

Therefore, if freedom of choice is able to be abused, then it can have bad consequences. Living in a world that is affected by the decisions people make and the imperfections that come along with them, it might become a little bit clearer as to why God does not heal everyone immediately. What would free will be if the consequences of free will never came to be? The obvious objection is that things that cause pain and bad consequences like murder should be stopped in their tracks. However, free will is not the type of thing that can be filtered based on the potential consequences. If people are free to make the right decision, like not murdering someone else, they need to be free to make the wrong decision. If God somehow predetermined all of these actions or did not allow the consequences of actions to occur, people would not be free. Also, unintended consequences can bring good from evil or evil from good actions. Therefore, humans would not even be free to act in morally good ways because sometimes a good deed causes someone else to suffer. Removing the consequences from free will decimates free will itself.

Allowing human free will applies to disability as well. God could alter the genetic code. God could prevent accidents from happening. As an omnipotent God, He certainly has that ability. However, if disability is a consequence of evil in the world as has been suggested, and if evil is a result of free will, then it would not be possible for God to remove all consequences without violating the free will of the creatures that He created to be free. God is omnipotent, but even God cannot create logical contradictions. He cannot make a square circle or a married bachelor. Similarly, God cannot make free, unfree creatures.

The question then advances to miracles, however. If it is true that God cannot systematically eliminate all bad things from happening in the world, including the consequences of evil that have corrupted the world from the fall, then why did Jesus heal some people? At the very least, limited healing does not seem to be fair. There have been millions of people with disabilities throughout history, and while Jesus healed many people, there were a lot more that He did not heal. The previous paragraphs about God violating free will seem to be a problem here as well. Wouldn't any miraculous healing be a problem for free will?

To take the first question first, when Jesus speaks about performing miracles such as healing a man born blind or raising Lazarus from the dead, it is always in the context of bringing glory to God. Therefore, there is a subtle difference between eliminating all evil *carte blanche* and healing with a particular purpose. In the first scenario, eliminating all consequences of evil simply to eliminate the consequences of evil implies that freedom is being restricted. In the second scenario, healing for a particular purpose does indeed eliminate a specific consequence of evil in the world, but it is no longer a question of freedom. Miracles did not take place to eliminate all evil *carte blanche* and therefore remove all free will.

Differentiating between eliminating all evil and eliminating a particular evil might seem essentially the same. However, as an illustration, consider a child who has the freedom to touch a hot burner. It is not that the parents want their child to touch the hot burner, but it sometimes happens because of the child's choice. The parents then have two potential responses. The parents can let the child suffer as a natural consequence of touching the hot burner. The parents can also apply medicine to help soothe the pain. In the second option, the parents are interfering with the natural consequence of suffering. However, it is not impinging on the child's free will, but it is providing an exception to the consequence by reducing the pain.

The illustration is not perfect because, as it has already been established multiple times, disability is not related to the person's individual sins, but it does demonstrate the difference between eliminating all consequences and bringing healing. However, the ultimate question is still open. If any parent would apply that medicine into the burned hand of the child to alleviate suffering, why does God not simply eliminate all disability?

It is wise to consider providence in this situation. As stated by Thomas Oden, "Faith in divine providence is the trust that God is silently working out the divine purpose through the historical process, even when we cannot fully recognize it, and that whatever the distortions and disruptions of history, God's purpose will be accomplished in the long run."[6] God is not silent. God has created a world where there is the potential of evil. However, that does not mean God does not act in the world. God does not violate free will, His own good gift to humanity. God can, however, provide the medicine. God can bring about healing to a world already broken by sin. If disability is a consequence of sin, then God can bring about healing, or God can use disability for His glory on earth.

For instance, consider the soul-making theodicy of Swinburne. There can be values that only develop through difficult times. Eareckson Tada testifies to this powerfully in the hypothetical conversation that she imagines she will have with God when she ultimately arrives in heaven.

> And then I will say, "Lord Jesus, do you see that wheelchair over there? Well, you were right. When you put me in it, it was a lot of trouble. But the weaker I was in that thing, the harder I leaned on you. And the harder I leaned on you, the stronger I discovered you to be. I do not think I would ever have known the glory of your grace were it not for the weakness of that wheelchair. So thank you, Lord Jesus, for that. Now, if you like, you can send that thing off to hell."[7]

Is it then possible that the ideal situation is not always healing? Is it possible that there are lives that can only be touched by people in certain situations? How many lives have been changed thanks to the ministry of Joni and Friends, which

---

6   Thomas C. Oden, *Classic Christianity* (New York: HarperCollins, 2009), 160, Kindle Edition.

7   Joni Eareckson Tada, "Wheelchairs in Heaven?" in *Why, O God?: Suffering and Disability in the Bible and the Church*, eds. Larry J. Waters and Roy B. Zuck (Wheaton: Crossway, 2001), Kindle Edition.

would not have started if Eareckson Tada herself had not had her accident? Some people might argue then that it was unreasonable of God to apply this burden to one lady in particular. After all, could there be an easier way for lives to be changed? Couldn't God have worked in the lives of those people in another way?

No one on earth knows every way God can change lives, but it is certainly possible that there would have been no other way for these lives to be changed. Assuming that God does everything in the best possible way, we live in the best possible world. If God could have done something better, then He would have. That seems to be the logical conclusion of understanding God's attributes as the problem of evil outlines. If God is all-good and all-powerful, then He would create the world that is the best. He would have the ability to do it and the moral compass to be able to do it. By supposing that God is not perfectly good and has not created the best possible world, the aforementioned question is not relevant concerning the problem of evil. The problem of evil is concerned with the perceived inconsistency between the attributes of God and the existence of evil. This question about God potentially being able to create a better world undermines the characteristics of God. However, it is not within the scope of the problem of evil. If God is not perfectly good or perfectly powerful, then there is no problem of evil. Given the premises, the world is as good as God could have possibly created it.

Overall, this might not seem to be very comforting then to people who have disabilities. Some will wonder if God is really good at His job. After all, if this world, which is cruel and often unjust, is the best that God could do, how could God truly be all-powerful? Again, this is still the wrong question to ask because if God is not all-powerful, the problem of evil is not a problem. Asking questions about God lacking power are irrelevant because they do not address the problem of evil. They seek to redefine the problem by using different premises. The problem of evil exists in the tension between all of these attributes. It would be somewhat like a Christian arguing that evil does not exist, so there is no problem of evil. Some people have argued along that line, but they are largely criticized because they are not addressing the problem of evil; they are going around it.

Therefore, why does God not eliminate disability? Under the presumption that this is the best possible world that God could create given the fact that God is good and therefore would create the best possible world, disability exists as a consequence of evil. Although some would argue to the contrary, lacking bodily function is not the way that humanity was created. Eyes were always meant to see. Muscles were always meant to flex and stretch. Therefore, disability would be a consequence of evil in a world that is imperfect. Acknowledging proper function does not demean individuals with disabilities; Christians universally believe that no one is perfect, and everyone has been affected in different ways by the world's imperfections.

The problem of evil needs to go back one level then. The question becomes why the world is created in such a way that evil could exist. If this is the best possible world that God could create, then by looking at some of the good attributes of this world, perhaps one will be a great enough good to justify the potential existence of evil. This is where the free will defense applies. It is essential to recognize that free will is a necessary precondition for relationships. A relationship can only be valuable if the other party wants to be a part of it. In European history, it was popular to arrange marriages for political purposes, but that did not guarantee healthy relationships. Perhaps the Prince and Princess were not compatible with each other. They were married, but they did not have a relationship because they had not chosen to develop that relationship. It came from outside themselves.

If it is the case that free will enables the possibility of relationship, the relationship between God and man would need to operate in the same way. If it is good for God to have a relationship with man, man needs to have the freedom to reject God. Robots cannot have a relationship. It might seem strange for God to allow people the freedom to reject Him, but if the possibility of relationships and love were a great enough good, then that could be a possible reason why God might allow for the possibility of the abuse of free will and the consequences that follow.

It is also worth considering that God is love. If God is love, then love is good. If love is good, then when God allowed humans to have the capability of loving, God did something good. Even though it is possible for humans to abuse love and corrupt it into a twisted perversion of itself, love is good. In fact, love in the purest sense is perfect. Love requires an object, and requiring an object necessitates a relationship. Relationship then requires the free will to enter into that relationship, or else it is the equivalent of an arranged marriage.

Finally, it is possible to return to the beginning of this argument and defend the simultaneous existence of the Christian God and disability. Disability is a consequence of evil. Disability does not show anything additionally evil about a person who has a disability, according to the Biblical testimony. In fact, the Biblical testimony indicates that everyone is evil and fallen yet is gloriously made in the image of God. The works of many theologians over the centuries interpret the Biblical evidence in the same way. They recognize that the Bible is a document that speaks about the equality of all before God and the necessity of salvation for all. In terms of innate value, disability does not make a difference; it does not make anyone more or less sinful or human.

After understanding the broken human condition, the question then becomes why God would allow the consequences of evil. The claim made by the free will defense is that the existence of evil is not inconsistent with the characteristics of the Christian God. The problem of evil has been reformulated for the purposes of this book to suggest that allowing the consequences of evil is not inconsistent with the characteristics of God. Disability is a consequence of evil rather than evil itself because, at the most basic level, disability is lacking certain abilities that humans were created to have and enjoy using. Lacking ability does not make disability evil, but in the sense that the entire world is fallen, the human body was affected by the fall as well. This fallenness can manifest itself in terms of moral evil or natural evil. The existence of a genetic disorder, natural evil, or the existence of a drunk driver ramming another motorist, moral evil, are both the consequences of human free will breaking what was a perfect world.

Therefore, even though the consequences of the fall might be more evident in people who have particularly physical disabilities that can be seen, the approach to answering this modified problem of the consequences of evil is not very much different than solving any problem of evil. The free will defense seems to make the most sense.

The free will defense emphasizes that humans are responsible for their condition. Humans have willfully rebelled against God, and, as a result, there are consequences to the decisions that humans have made. If disability truly is a consequence of evil and if God truly did create the best world possible, then God allows disability for the same reason. Therefore, free will would need to be a great enough good to justify the risk of evil entering the world. Free will allows for love and relationships with both God and other people, as well as the possibility that it would be abused. It makes sense that robots would not be very rewarding to have a relationship with or to receive glory from, so God's motivation for allowing evil very well could have been free will as a very great good. If it is possible free will was a great enough good for God to allow the possibility of evil, then the logical problem of evil is solved. The consequence of evil that is disability is simply another part of that abuse; it is not a particularly difficult or problematic part of the equation. The differentiation between moral evil and natural evil is not of great consequence from a free will perspective. Evil, in all of its variations, exists because of the human abuse of free will. Had humans not abused free will, evil would not exist, and the consequences of evil, like disability, would not exist.

A soul-making theodicy also has potential value. It points out that God can use disability for good purposes. It actually can be reconciled with the free will defense on one particular point. Even if this chapter's defense assumes that disability is a consequence of evil brought on by the human abuse of free will, God's providence can help people who have to live in a fallen world develop beneficial characteristics such as courage, perseverance, and strength. In that sense, then, it does not mean God brought about disability only to develop human souls, but because of the reality of evil in the world, God works within the framework that He established to not violate free will and simultaneously bring about good from bad situations. The soul-making theodicy espoused by Swinburne comes along with the problematic assumption that God is not aware of the future, though. Hence, it is not quite as powerful as the straightforward free will defense of Plantinga or its derivation presented in this chapter. In this reformulated free will defense, free will and the possibility of a relationship with God are elevated to a very high level as great enough goods to justify free will's abuse.

The existence of disability is not a knockout punch to a belief in the existence of the Christian God. Instead, there are good reasons for believing that even though disability might be a consequence of the evil in the world, there are reasons that God might have for allowing the possibility of evil to exist. Free will itself seems to be the most compelling reason for evil and its consequences to exist. If it is true that humanity was created to bring glory to God and have a relationship with Him, then humanity needs to have the ability to reject God. That possibility of rejection requires freedom, but freedom is not a negative. On the contrary, it allows us to enter into a loving relationship with God and therefore enjoy Him, not only in this life but in the life to come. Does that mean that there will be consequences of evil in this world? Certainly. Does that mean that disability exists because of this freedom? Yes, it does. To quote again from Joni Eareckson Tada, a relationship with God is worth all the struggles. "If the cross can be seen not as a symbol of torture but as a symbol of hope and life, then a wheelchair can be 'redeemed' from a symbol of confinement to a representation of an intimate fellowship with the Lord Jesus Christ."[8] However, as the book of James compellingly reminds us, our lives on earth are like a vapor.[9] No matter what situation we find ourselves in, if the claims of Christianity are true, earthly suffering is nothing compared to the eternal joy that awaits those who have entered into a freely chosen relationship with God. That is the promise of Revelation, the promise of the Bible at large, and the promise of God Himself.

---

8   Joni Eareckson Tada, "Redeeming Suffering," in *Why, O God?: Suffering and Disability in the Bible and the Church*, eds. Larry J. Waters and Roy B. Zuck (Wheaton: Crossway, 2001), Kindle Edition.

9   James 4:14, ESV.

Conclusion

This book began by speaking about the existence of difficulty. There is no doubt that many people live through painful experiences. Many problems occur, and some of them are more significant than others. Living life with a disability is not easy. At the most basic level, disabilities are limitations on particular abilities. For people with physical disabilities, mobility might be a challenge. For people with intellectual disabilities, academics might be more difficult. That is the undeniable situation of living a life with a disability. Even with all of the accommodations that the modern world can provide, limitations still exist, and they still create circumstances that some people are eager to use to condemn God.

Many people are quick to ask how God could possibly allow something like disability to exist. They might argue that it is not fair for certain people to have to fight certain battles. They might say that God is twisted and cruel for allowing circumstances to come into people's lives and experience difficulty levels that seem to be above and beyond those of most of the rest of the population. The purpose of this work has been to, first of all, explore the consistent Christian testimony on what disability actually means but, more importantly, to explain why disability does not disprove the existence of the Christian God. Specifically, it argues that there is no inconsistency between the existence of disability and the existence of God.

By mainly drawing on the free will defense, it has been shown that it is possible for God to have a reason for allowing disability to exist in the world. It has been posited that the ultimate good of free will is enough of a benefit to humanity to allow for the possibility that rebellion against God could occur. Through free will, relationships and love are possible. By granting humans free will, God does not simply have a planet full of robots, but He has created beings that can truly worship Him and connect with each other. It has been argued that free will meets the criteria of being a greater good than the amount of evil in the world. If that is true, then it is reasonable to believe that God did create the best world possible. However, that world was corrupted morally and naturally by the choices of free agents and is still experiencing the consequences of evil. Everything in the world is corrupted by the fall, and both natural and moral evil exist because of it. An example of natural evil can be seen in the changes in the genetic code that allow for mutations and subsequent disabilities. Moral evil can be seen in people who drive their cars while intoxicated and crash into other people who then face the challenges of spinal cord injuries. Both kinds of evil are the consequence of humanity's sinful choices and abuse of the good gift of free will. It is not that people with disabilities are inherently any more evil than anyone else on earth because all have sinned and fall short of the glory of God.[1] Rather, just like everyone else, they live in a world full of the consequences of evil, and those consequences manifest themselves differently for different people.

If that is true, then it should be clear that asking the question as to why God does not miraculously heal people all the time and eliminate disability once and for all is simply a subset of the problem of evil with slight modifications. If free will is a great enough good, then disability was part of the potential consequence of evil that came from allowing people to have free will. It was a good gift that was abused, and the world has never been the same since. Humans were no longer able to have the same type of relationship with God that had been in place previously. Remember, however, that if free will is a great enough good, then the existence of disability does not disprove the existence of God. Instead, in creating the best possible world, God allowed for free will, and free agents created a problem that still bears fruit today. God did not and does not create evil.

This conclusion might not provide very much consolation for people with disabilities. It seems too philosophical to be of any comfort to someone living a life where he or she is not happy with the reality of disability. However, please keep in mind that this is not meant to be a pastoral book. Rather, the question of why God allows disability is, at heart, a logical question. To phrase it in the terms suggested at the beginning of this book, it deals with moral and natural evil, and it is mostly concerned with the personal problem of evil, the doctrinal problem of evil, and the apologetic problem of evil. The problem of evil attempts to show an inconsistency between the existence of disability in the world and the existence of an all-good, all-powerful, and all-knowing God overseeing the world. Therefore, the answer has to be philosophical in nature, or it will not address the actual problem of evil. That is the doctrinal part, and the ability to communicate that is the apologetic part. Because disability has an impact on the individual level, that is certainly a personal problem of evil.

The pastoral problem is very important, and it is a potential area for more research on Christianity and disability. Much more could be written about different pastoral approaches to handling the problem of evil to comfort people with disabilities, family members, or society at large. For example, since philosophical answers might not be comforting to every person, sometimes there is no greater testimony than to be present and to weep with those who are weeping. Jesus Himself did that at the death of Lazarus even though He knew that He was going to raise Lazarus from the dead.[2] Another pastoral answer to the problem of evil is to help break down environmental and attitudinal barriers people with disabilities face. Jacober calls the church not just to allow the attendance of individuals with disabilities but rather to embrace the entire body of Christ actively. She writes, "Valuing the role of every member as equal is

---

1   Romans 3:23, ESV.

2   John 11:35, ESV.

itself a bold move toward truly being the body of Christ. It is no longer acceptable to be welcoming and allow someone to sit in your space as a permanent visitor who is able to observe but never partake in or give back to the community."[3] When a person needs to use a wheelchair after an injury, changes will probably be needed at his or her house. Churches should be the first in line to help people create accessible living spaces. Although renovation might not provide the type of spiritual guidance that the pastoral problem of evil seems to require, often, to use a cliché, actions really do speak louder than words. By showing people that others care and are willing to help, even though there might be evil in the world, it becomes evident that there are also loving and caring people willing to lend a hand. With all the changes that might be going on in a person's life, supports can help address the pastoral problem of evil.

In the history of Christianity, many attacks have been brought from all angles to try to show that God is anything but who He says He is. Satan tempted Adam and Eve and promised them that they could be like God.[4] What they should have known, and surely what Satan himself knew, was that there was no possibility that they could ever be like God. God is not someone who can be replicated, but often, people want to climb into the driver's seat. They want to say that there is no possible way for God to have created the world in a particular way. They argue that God could not possibly have allowed disability because that would, necessarily, make the world an unjust and unfair place. However, what they do not realize is that they are not capable of taking over the controls from God. It is not possible for a person to become God, and the Bible is very clear about that. Therefore, even though it is popular to throw around accusations about the goodness of God and claim that there is no possible way for God to be who He said He is and allow the consequences of evil in the world like disability, that claim simply does not hold up to the scrutiny of logic. Rather, it is perfectly consistent to claim that God does exist, has exactly the qualities He claimed to have, and simultaneously had a reason for allowing things that are perceived to be evil in the world. The goodness of free will and the benefits associated with it outweigh the consequences associated with the abuse of free will, including, but not limited to, disability.

As this book draws to its conclusion, I cannot help but remember the recently released documentary entitled "Crip Camp." Released in the middle of a time of isolation, its message of community resonated with audiences and critics alike. What begins as an inside look at a hippie summer camp for kids with disabilities in upstate New York evolves into a story about the struggles that many of the same individuals who came together at summer camp went through as they fought the United States government for what ultimately turned out to be the Americans

---

3   Amy E. Jacober, *Redefining Perfect: The Interplay Between Theology and Disability* (Eugene, OR: Cascade Books, 2017), chap. 6, Kindle Edition.

4   Genesis 3:5, ESV.

with Disabilities Act. One cannot help but be impressed by the accomplishment of the alumni of this camp as they changed the lives of people with disabilities for the better.

While faith plays almost no role in this film, the consistent theme that does echo through the story is the recognition that people with disabilities are people. For example, in his review for *The New York Times*, Ben Kenisberg writes, "Ultimately, 'Crip Camp' has a universal message: Inspirations that begin in youth can lead to radical, world-changing results."[5] Brian Tallerico, reviewing the film for *RogerEbert.com*, similarly praised the film, saying, "With deep film making empathy that strikes a remarkable balance between delivering a universal message and telling very individual stories, 'Crip Camp' offers something we could all use more of — hope for the future."[6] Both point to a universal message about the importance of hope and the humanity of those who experience evil.

I hope the same themes of humanity and hopefulness will emanate from this book as you consider and reflect on the relationship between disability and the problem of evil. I do believe that disability exists and entered the world at the same time as evil, a consequence of Adam and Eve's sin. My position may seem to be much less hopeful than the tone struck by "Crip Camp." However, for the Christian, the ultimate hope of the world was delivered in the person of Jesus Christ. Being a member of the human race, a privileged species created in the image of God, with the ability to have a relationship with our Creator, is a blessing unsurpassed in the remainder of the universe. Some question the existence of this Creator because of the barriers they have experienced in their own lives, and if this book has done anything to help lower those defenses and open someone's heart to the possibility that Christianity might be true and God may be everything that He says He is despite the existence of disability, then I can't help but think that it might change the world.

---

5   Ben Kenigsberg, "'Crip Camp' Review: After Those Summers, Nothing Was the Same," *The New York Times*, March 24, 2020, accessed December 28, 2020, https://www. nytimes.com/2020/03/24/movies/crip-camp-review.html.

6   Brian Tallerico, "Crip Camp: A Disability Revolution," *RogerEbert.com*, March 25, 2020, accessed December 28, 2020, https://www.rogerebert.com/reviews/crip-camp-a-disability-revolution-movie-review-2020.

Bibliography

"A Guide to Disability Rights Laws." United States Department of Justice, Civil Rights Division. Last modified July 2009. Accessed March 5, 2016. http://www.ada.gov/cguide.htm.

Anderson, Owen. "Free Will and Doxological Christianity." *DrOwenAnderson.com.* October 31, 2020. Accessed December 28, 2020. https://drowenanderson.com/free-will-and-doxological-christianity/.

——––. *Job: A Philosophical Commentary*. Phoenix: Logos Papers Press, 2021.

Bayes, Ros. "A Biblical View of Disability." *BeThinking.* 2015. Accessed December 28, 2020. https://www.bethinking.org/human-life/a-biblical-view-of-disability.

Belser, Julia Watts, and Melanie S. Morrison. "What No Longer Serves Us: Resisting Ableism and Anti-Judaism in New Testament Healing Narratives." *Journal of Feminist Studies in Religion* 27, no. 2 (2011): 153-70. Accessed November 26, 2020. doi:10.2979/jfemistudreli.27.2.153.

Brock, Brian, and John Swinton, eds. *Disability in the Christian Tradition*. Grand Rapids: Wm. B. Eerdmans, 2012. Kindle Edition.

Broesterhuizen, Marcel. "A Liberating Approach to Human Contingency." *Gregorianum* 89, no. 1 (2008): 150-67. Accessed November 26, 2020. http://www.jstor.org/stable/23582110.

Bruce, Patricia. "Constructions of Disability (Ancient and Modern): The Impact of Religious Beliefs on the Experience of Disability." *Neotestamentica* 44, no. 2 (2010): 253-81. Accessed November 26, 2020. http://www.jstor.org/stable/43048759.

Creamer, Deborah Beth. "Embracing Limits, Queering Embodiment: Creating/Creative Possibilities for Disability Theology." *Journal of Feminist Studies in Religion* 26, no. 2 (2010): 123-27. Accessed November 26, 2020. doi:10.2979/fsr.2010.26.2.123.

"disability, n." *OED Online.* Last modified September 2020 Accessed November 26, 2020. https://www.oed.com/view/Entry/53381?redirectedFrom=disability+.

"Disability Employment Statistics." *United States Department of Labor.* Accessed December 28, 2020. https://www.dol.gov/agencies/odep/research/statistics.

Evans, Jeremy A. *The Problem of Evil: The Challenge to Essential Christian Beliefs.* Nashville: B&H Academic, 2013. Kindle Edition.

"Frequently Asked Questions (FAQs)." *United Nations Enable.* Last modified 2007. Accessed March 5, 2016. http://www.un.org/esa/socdev/enable/faqs.htm.

Gangadean, Surrendra. *Philosophical Foundation: A Critical Analysis of Basic Beliefs.* Lanham, MD: University Press of America, 2008.

Hardwick, Lamar. *Disability and the Church.* Downers Grove, IL: InterVarsity Press, 2021. Kindle Edition.

Hart, David Bentley. *The Doors of the Sea: Where Was God in the Tsunami?* Grand Rapids: Wm. B. Eerdmans, 2005. Kindle Edition.

Heumann, Judith, and John Wodatch. "We're 20 Percent of America, and We're Still Invisible." *The New York Times.* July 26, 2020. Accessed April 20, 2021. https://www.nytimes.com/2020/07/26/opinion/Americans-with-disabilities-act.html.

Hicks, Josh. "Puerto Ricans who can't speak English qualify as disabled for Social Security." *The Washington Post.* April 10, 2015. Accessed March 5, 2016. https://www.washingtonpost.com/news/federal-eye/wp/2015/04/10/puerto-ricans-who-cant-speak-english-qualify-as-disabled-for-social-security/.

Hitchens Christopher, ed. *The Portable Atheist.* Philadelphia: Da Capo Press, 2007. Kindle Edition.

Hume, David. *Dialogues Concerning Natural Religion.* Edited by Richard H. Popkin. Indianapolis: Hackett Publishing Company, 1998. Kindle Edition.

"Interview: 'Down Syndrome is not a Disease, but Another Personal Characteristic.'" *Disability World.* Accessed April 7, 2016. http://www.disabilityworld.org/06-08_03/il/down.shtml.

Jacober, Amy E. *Redefining Perfect: The Interplay Between Theology and Disability.* Eugene, OR: Cascade Books, 2017. Kindle Edition.

Kaplan, Deborah. "The Definition of Disability." *The Center for An Accessible Society.* Accessed December 28, 2020. http://www.accessiblesociety.org/topics/demographics-identity/dkaplanpaper.htm.

Keener, Craig S. Miracles: *The Credibility of the New Testament.* Grand Rapids: Baker Academic, 2011. Kindle Edition.

Kenigsberg, Ben. "'Crip Camp' Review: After Those Summers, Nothing Was the Same." *The New York Times*. March 24, 2020. Accessed December 28, 2020. https://www.nytimes.com/2020/03/24/movies/crip-camp-review.html.

Lukianoff, Greg, and Jonathan Haidt. *The Coddling of the American Mind*. New York: Penguin Press, 2018. Kindle Edition.

Mackie, J.L. "Evil and Omnipotence." *Mind* 64, No. 254 (April 1955): 200-212. Accessed March 5, 2016. http://www.jstor.org/stable/2251467.

"Meet the 'Spiritual but Not Religious.'" *Barna*. April 6, 2017. Accessed December 28, 2020. https://www.barna.com/research/meet-spiritual-not-religious/.

Miles, M. "Martin Luther and Childhood Disability in 16th Century Germany: What did he write? What did he say?" *Independent Living Institute*. 2005. Accessed December 28, 2020. https://www.independentliving.org/docs7/miles2005b.html.

Oden, Thomas C. *Classic Christianity*. New York: HarperCollins, 2009. Kindle Edition.

Plantinga, Alvin. *God, Freedom, and Evil*. Grand Rapids: Wm. B. Eerdmans, 1977. Kindle Edition.

Rigney, Joe. "Confronting the Problem(s) of Evil." *Desiring God*. December 15, 2012. Accessed December 28, 2020. https://www.desiringgod.org/articles/confronting-the-problems-of-evil.

Schmoll, Zak. "A Silent Genocide: Disability and the Ongoing Consequences of Social Darwinism." In*An Unexpected Journal: Image Bearers* 4, no. 1 (Spring 2021). March 10, 2021. Accessed April 24, 2021. https://anunexpectedjournal.com/a-silent-genocide-disability-and-the-ongoing-consequences-of-social-darwinism/.

Schumm, Darla Y. "Reimaging Disability." *Journal of Feminist Studies in Religion* 26, no. 2 (2010): 132-37. Accessed November 26, 2020. doi:10.2979/fsr.2010.26.2.132.

Swinburne, Richard. *Providence and the Problem of Evil*. New York: Oxford University Press, 1998. Kindle Edition.

Tallerico, Brian. "Crip Camp: A Disability Revolution." *RogerEbert.com*. March 25, 2020. Accessed December 28, 2020. https://www.rogerebert.com/reviews/crip-camp-a-disability-revolution-movie-review-2020.

"The Westminster Confession of Faith (1647)." *Ligonier Ministries*. Accessed December 28, 2020. https://www.ligonier.org/learn/articles/westminster-confession-faith/.

Trueman, Carl R. *The Rise and Triumph of the Modern Self*. Wheaton: Crossway, 2020. Kindle Edition.

van Inwagen, Peter. *The Problem of Evil*. New York: Oxford University Press, 2006. Kindle Edition.

Waters, Larry J., and Roy B. Zuck, eds. *Why, O God?: Suffering and Disability in the Bible and the Church*. Wheaton: Crossway, 2001. Kindle Edition.

"Wrath and Grace Radio | Disabilities and the Church." *YouTube*. March 22, 2020. Accessed April 25, 2021. https://www.youtube.com/watch?v=g9av0QyPrzU.

Yong, Amos. *The Bible, Disability, and the Church: A New Vision of the People of God*. Grand Rapids: Wm. B Eerdmans, 2011. Kindle Edition.